new light
on the Gospels

Cover illustration: a crystal

Omraam Mikhaël Aïvanhov

new light on the Gospels

Translated from the French

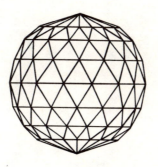

Collection Izvor
No. 217

EDITIONS PROSVETA

By the same author:
(translated from the French)

Izvor Collection

201 - Toward a Solar Civilisation
202 - Man, Master of his Destiny
203 - Education Begins Before Birth
204 - The Yoga of Nutrition
205 - Sexual Force or the Winged Dragon
206 - The Universal White Brotherhood is not a Sect
207 - What is a Spiritual Master?
208 - Under the Dove, the Reign of Peace
209 - Christmas and Easter in the Initiatic Tradition
210 - The Tree of the Knowledge of Good and Evil
211 - Freedom, the Spirit Triumphant
212 - Light is a Living Spirit
213 - Man's Two Natures: Human and Divine
214 - Hope for the World: Spiritual Galvanoplasty
215 - The True Meaning of Christ's Teaching
216 - The Living Book of Nature

© 1985 by Prosveta S.A. – B.P. 12 – F-83601 Fréjus
ALL RIGHTS RESERVED

ISBN 2-85566-339-3
édition originale : ISBN 2-85566-284-2

TABLE OF CONTENTS

1   "Men do not put new wine into old bottles" 11

2   "Except ye become as little children" . 25

3   The unjust steward 47

4   "Lay up for yourselves treasures in heaven" 73

5   The strait gate 87

6   "Let him which is on the housetop not come down..." 95

7   The calming of the storm 109

8   The first shall be last 117

9   The parable of the five wise and the five foolish virgins 135

10   "This is life eternal, that they might know Thee the only true God" . 161

EDITOR'S NOTE

The reader is asked to bear in mind that the Editors have retained the spoken style of the Master Omraam Mikhaël Aïvanhov in his presentation of the Teaching of the great Universal White Brotherhood, the essence of the Teaching being the spoken Word.

They also wish to clarify the point that the word *white* in Universal White Brotherhood does not refer to colour or race, but to purity of soul. The Teaching shows how all men without exception (universal), can live a new form of life on earth (brotherhood), in harmony (white) and with respect for each other's race, creed and country... that is, Universal White Brotherhood.

1

"MEN DO NOT PUT NEW WINE INTO OLD BOTTLES"

"No man putteth a piece of new cloth unto an old garment, for that which is put in to fill it up taketh from the garment, and the rent is made worse. Neither do men put new wine into old bottles: else the bottles break, and the wine runneth out and the bottles perish: but they put new wine into new bottles, and both are preserved."

St. Matthew 9: 16, 17.

You will have heard these verses quoted many times yet, despite this, I think that you have very little idea of the truth contained within this passage and I feel that you ought to know these truths. What is meant by 'old' and 'new' bottles and by 'new wine' itself? Nowadays, wine is put in vats, but in the past they used leather bottles made out of animal skins stitched into sacs. It was not possible to put new wine into old wineskins because wine produces all sorts of fermentation and releases gasses which would destroy second-hand skins and so the wine would have spilled and been wasted. Therefore new wine was put into new skins which were strong and capable of resisting very great pressure.

Let us look at this process of fermentation from the scientific point of view. It is a natural decomposition of organic matter. There are different forms of fermentation and some, in particular, have been studied by alchemists, for they supply the necessary elements to make the philosopher's stone. Many types of fermentation can also take place in man, not only in his physical organs, but also in his thoughts and feelings.

When Jesus said, "They put new wine into new bottles, and both are preserved," he was comparing his teaching to new wine, and saying that this teaching must be poured into solid, resistant beings, capable of accepting all the changes which would inevitably take place in them. Initiatic teaching, just like wine, is no dead thing; on the contrary, it is alive, and it is that very life which causes all sorts of consequences. The wineskin Jesus talked of symbolizes man, and within this skin you can find many other sacs: the head, the lungs, the stomach... the heart, the intellect and the soul are also wineskins and if one does not pay attention to what is put into them or does not look after the condition of the skins, the results are disastrous.

Sometimes people come complaining to me saying, "Before I met this Teaching I felt so very much better: I ate and drank and did all sorts of stupid things. I had a great time and I felt marvellous. But, since I decided to try and follow this Teaching of the Universal White Brotherhood, I feel slightly uncomfortable all the time, as if something is beginning to bubble away inside me. I really don't think that this Teaching suits me." They have no understanding of what is going on within and so, instead of allowing this normal evolution to take place, they weep and get discouraged and withdraw. How do I view this attitude? I say that they are old skins in which it is still too soon to pour new wine!

Watch yourself and watch others. You will see that once a Teaching, however divine, has been accepted, at the end of a month perhaps, or six months, or a year (depending on the individual), you will notice that people start behaving in most contradictory ways. They become irritable and depressed and, far from intensifying the positive side in them, their work only develops the negative side because each new thought, each new feeling produces even more fermentation within.

Hearing this, you may well think that it is very dangerous to accept our Teaching, even though it really is so pure and divine. I assure you that there is no danger whatsoever, but first of all you must know one thing: you must prepare a strong enough structure in yourself to contain and support such a philosophy, such an idea, such a new teaching. You cannot receive a new philosophy without first harmonizing with it, without first preparing and fortifying your stomach, your head, your lungs, in fact all your organism, so that it will be able to resist the tension produced by the new currents you will receive. Do not delude yourself that the currents of love and light are easy to bear. In fact, I would say that people are better able to support suffering, pain and disappointment than they can joy, inspiration and very high energy. Often you could say that people even like to be immersed in complications and that if one day they were to receive a luminous inspiration, they would do everything possible to get rid of it. Why do people behave like this when it is such a very rare and precious gift to receive divine inspiration?

If only people had an idea of what physiological, chemical and psychological improvements take place in the presence of a divine idea! Yet it is precisely this presence they push away from themselves and, if they continue to do so they will never find the same opportunities to transform themselves. One day they will regret having acted in this way and will say, "How true: I chased away the light so many times because I was afraid of having the Spirit within me!" I have often noticed that people are much more afraid of the Spirit and sublime states of consciousness than they are of Hell and all its devils, of suffering, disorder, and all those lower states of being. In a way they have a point because somewhere within them they are aware that they are not new wineskins and so, instinctively, they are afraid of being unable to bear this new life, this new expansion of their consciousness, and also they still feel the need to lead life at a lower level. Those who fear the life of the Spirit do not really know why they fear it but feel, instinctively, that there is something to fear: they will have to give up their old habits. In reality, there is nothing more beautiful than to be able to grasp the spiritual currents of light, strength and joy which come daily to us, to receive this love which constantly transpierces our souls. If we block these currents because of our weaknesses, our thoughts and our negative feelings, it shows that our wineskins are not yet ready to receive the new wine. We have old skins and we must change them. The cells of the body are constantly renewed. Each day old and sickly cells are replaced by new and healthy ones. This process of renewal works in a seven year cycle during which all the molecules and atoms of our bodies are replaced by others. In that case, I hear you argue, the renewal is complete! Not so, because even if all our cells have been replaced, you must realize that each cell has a memory and so is able to transmit etheric imprints of old habits on to the new cells. Thanks to these imprints, thoughts, feelings and energies circulate in these old, well-traced furrows... which explains why the new particles inherit the memory of the old particles and, despite the fact that seven years have rolled by, the cells still remain in the same or, often, in a much worse condition.

How old are you? How many seven-year cycles have you already lived through? Yet aren't you still loyal to the same old habits; still thinking in the same old way, and still doing the same stupid things? However much your cells may have regenerated every seven years, the essential you has not been affected or changed. Your body may be transformed but your tendencies, your habits, stay exactly the same because the new particles have been imprinted by old patterns and old memories.

If you are to achieve real self-transformation, you must change the memories of your cells. As fast as the new cells come in, you must impreg-

"Men do not put new wine into old bottles" 17

nate them with new thoughts and with new feelings. Yes, if you are really conscious, you can renew the wineskins as fast as you pour in the new wine of a spiritual teaching. Otherwise, if you go on living in the same disorder and with the same dangerous habits, fermentation will take place in the wineskins. For this reason, as we receive this spiritual teaching, we must at the same time transform the memory of our cells. This we do by consciously introducing new elements into ourselves, watching over the purity of the food, drink and air we take in and scrutinizing all we absorb, both visible and invisible. Then, and then alone, we can receive a new philosophy and new spiritual currents without the slightest trace of fear.

Having spoken about wineskins, let us now speak of wine. Nearly all of you drink wine and, taken in small quantities, it is not harmful. Some people even say that wine fills them with inspiration! However, as you know, adulterated wines do exist and it is much better for you not to drink them because they have been prepared with all sorts of very harmful ingredients which I shall not detail here. What I want to point out to you is that the same phenomenon occurs on the spiritual plane as on the physical plane. You will find teachings and philosophical systems which are similar to these adulterated wines: they are made out of a heterogenous collection of ingredients which have nothing living or substantial at the heart of them. When you have drunk of this wine you feel disturbed, upset and ill. So, instead of going to buy your wine in any old shop, the secret is to make your own wine for your own consumption... your own wine brewed from your own thoughts, feelings and actions. Of course, you immediately question whether this wine which I am pouring in to your wineskins is an adulterated wine. You are welcome to think what you like! My advice to you is to suggest that you plant a vine in your soul, cultivate it, pick its grapes, crush them and then drink their juice. You can drink as much as you like of this good wine which you have made yourself; you can even get drunk on it!

This image of pouring new wine into new skins symbolizes the union of spirit and matter and, when I speak of matter, I mean not just physical matter but psychic matter: the very stuff of your thoughts and feelings. You cannot stay happy just pouring the Teaching into your head, stuffing yourself each day with new ideas, without at the same time renewing your physical and psychic being by living a life of increasing purity. If you stop yourself from learning this new way of living, the wineskins, stretched to

"Men do not put new wine into old bottles" 19

bursting, will soon explode because their material cannot take the strain of the new forces they are receiving. If you do not do your breathing exercises, if you do not do the gymnastics, if you do not pray, meditate, eat and live according to the rules of the new Teaching, then do not be surprised if all sorts of anomalies appear. When the fermentation begins you will feel so troubled and nervous that you will clash with everybody. I have seen men who, once they embraced the spiritual life, became exaggeratedly irritable towards their wives and children. A spiritual Teaching should not provoke such reactions, and signs of such fermentation prove that the wineskins are too old and worn out!

I know that some of you are thinking right now: "That's all very well, we have understood that a marvellous teaching exists. We need to evolve, we have an enormous amount of work to do, that's certain. However we do not know how to set about it. Give us the methods, because it is methods we lack." What you say is both true and false, for I have already given you many methods, but you have not really appreciated them; they seem so insignificant to you. You still go on waiting for the magic moment when I will reveal such sensational methods to you that you will instantly be transformed. What a pity! Such methods do not exist!

You will never find a true Initiate giving you recipes for instant wisdom, instant strength and instant liberation. Transformation of character is only possible by an uninterrupted round of daily work. If anybody says to you, "Use this formula, take this pentagram, follow this magical rite... and you will instantly be saved", you can be absolutely certain that he is lying because he has something to gain by deceiving you. A true Master will tell you, "Dear children, everything is possible, but only if you make the effort. Then, when you gave done so, what you obtain will be so deeply a part of you that no one will ever be able to take it away." Everything which you gain by instant methods, by magic spells, cannot be durable. Just a short while afterwards you will lose all that you thought you had achieved because it was not gained by personal effort.

There are Masters living who in an instant could develop all sorts of qualities in you, but they do not do it as they are aware that these virtues would not last. Love, knowledge, powers, cannot come from outside like wine poured into a bottle... it is we ourselves who must work each and every day to transform our wineskins. Unfortunately all the schools which demand personal effort from their candidates are not very successful, whereas those that promise amazing

"Men do not put new wine into old bottles" 21

effects without asking them to lift a finger are wildly popular! True teachings attract very few disciples.

Heaven is preparing to send powerful currents, rather like a new wine. Those who are not ready to take this wine of change will not be able to continue their existence, because the Invisible World will fill all skins, whether old or new. The time is coming when the Great Mysteries will be revealed to all. Humanity is made up of a mixture of old and new skins but, when the new wine arrives, that fact will be irrelevant: there will be no selection, all the skins will be filled. The new ones will be able to support the pressure and so will hold. Too bad if the old ones explode!

So, work each day at renewing your wineskins... by which I mean work on yourselves, work on all your cells, work on all your organs so that you will be ready to receive the new wine of those powerful and beneficial currents which the Invisible World is preparing to pour out on the world.

2

"EXCEPT YE BECOME AS LITTLE CHILDREN"

I

"And they brought young children to him, that he should touch them; and his disciples rebuked those that brought them. But when Jesus saw it, he was much displeased, and said unto them, Suffer the little children to come unto me, and forbid them not; for of such is the kingdom of God. Verily I say unto you, Whosoever shall not receive the kingdom of God as a little child, he shall not enter therein. And he took them up in his arms, put his hands upon them and blessed them."

St. Mark 10: 13-16.

"At the same time came the disciples unto Jesus, saying, Who is the greatest in the kingdom of heaven? And Jesus called a little child unto him, and set him in the midst of them and said, Verily I say unto you, Except ye be converted, and become as little children, ye shall not enter into the kingdom of heaven."

St. Matthew 18: 1-3.

Hearing me read this, you are undoubtedly wondering why I have chosen these particular verses. They have been quoted for two thousand years by churchmen and yet, despite being told to become like little children, man has made no progress. "Suffer the little children to come unto me, for of such is the kingdom of God".... "Except ye become as little children, ye shall not enter into the kingdom of heaven." However, when I explain these lines to you in the light of Initiatic tradition you will see that they contain some very profound ideas.

When you think of childhood, you cannot but think of old age, as there is a link between the two. Children are very drawn to old people who, in their turn, like children very much. Life is like a circle which begins with childhood and ends with old age and the two ends join each other. However, of course, a child and an old man do not inspire the same feelings in us at all. You long to hug and kiss a small child, to hold it in your arms and to jog it about on your knees... but you do not want to do that with an old man! Why do you think that is? If you say that a child is lighter, that does not answer the question!

The child is born with its hands clenched tightly shut, whereas the old man dies with his hands open. The clenched fist of the child says, "I have great confidence in my strength, I want

"Except ye become as little children" 27

to manifest myself, I want to conquer the entire world." The old man, however, who has wasted his life looking for a happiness he never found says, "I thought I would obtain so many things yet I have lost them all. I was deceived." He can no longer hold on to anything and so he opens his hands. Many people are disappointed at the end of their lives for, despite their great age, they have neither gained nor learned anything.

In fact, it is very difficult to become a true old man, so difficult that Jesus said, "Except ye become as little children, ye shall not enter into the Kingdom of God". In Heaven there are already the twenty-four Elders and therefore there is no room for any others. In the Revelation of St. John it is written, "And round about the throne were four and twenty seats: and upon the seats I saw four and twenty elders sitting, clothed in white raiment; and they had on their heads crowns of gold." The twenty-four Elders are extremely elevated beings. They form a council which presides over the destiny of men. How dare we presume to put ourselves forward as candidates for this council? So you see, since we cannot present ourselves in Paradise as old people, we must arrive as children! When we do that, the gates are opened freely... all children are accepted. Paradise is populated with children whereas there are only twenty-four Elders.

Don't you believe me? Why, the very fact that all the old people are sent back to reincarnate on earth proves that they are not wanted in Paradise! People say, "My father has gone to Heaven to be with God". In fact, he has already reincarnated as a tiny baby in some family. And if you wonder why he has come back, I will tell you that it is precisely to learn the love and wisdom that lie hidden in these two symbols of the child and the old man.

The child and the old man represent two virtues which we must learn to develop during our existence. The child represents love, which brings an abundance of forces and energies, which wants to see everything, touch everything, which wants to act and do everything possible in life. The old man represents the wisdom which observes, analyses, draws conclusions. The two must work together, however, because these days you can see that the tendency to develop the intellect at the expense of the heart is very prevalent and people have become critical and intolerant. Instead of showing wisdom they behave like grouchy old men, which is not the same thing at all!

Have you watched children when they are learning to walk? They fall down, clamber up, fall down again, scramble up again, until they have learnt to keep standing. Whereas if you see

"Except ye become as little children" 29

an old man encountering a difficulty or a check he says, "That's it, I'm not going to try again." If he falls down, he lies there, waiting for someone to come and pick him up; help is brought in the form of the ambulance to take him to hospital. So, if you are old in your character, soul and thoughts, when you fall down you don't get up. You lie there, saying weakly, "Others can get up and act, but my life and work are finished." Oh no, this is not the way to behave! You must keep on making efforts, thousands of them if necessary, but you must get up and start to walk, otherwise you will never learn to walk in the Kingdom of God.

Take another example from children's behavior: if you give them a sweet, a stone, an insect to look at, they will be so happy! Nothing, however, pleases old people; they always find something to grumble and complain about. That is why they will never enter the Kingdom of God, because the Kingdom of God is a state of consciousness based on flexibility and joy. If they are not capable of entering into the Kingdom of God during this life, how much less will they be able to when they get to the other side. From now on they will be refused entry.

When I talk in this way about old men do not think that I am just dealing with a question of age, because there are youngsters who at sixteen are already old inside: they are sombre, blasé, filled with cynicism and disgust, nothing has any appeal, not one single activity tempts them; they are incapable of aspirations or of feelings of wonder and enthusiasm. On the other hand, there are old people who have young, rich, inexhaustible hearts. You want to hug them because they are so radiant, joyful and delicious! Yes, in spite of their age, you long to hug them and carry them in your arms as they are the real children.

Children are carefree, they do not worry what the future will bring. The old torment themselves, continually worrying about tomorrow which they always see as full of uncertainty, sickness, misery and loneliness... and unfortunately modern culture encourages us to be old people with these thoughts. Apparently it is not very intelligent to be like children and the greatest insult is to treat someone like a child! If you want to impress public opinion, you have to look worried, bowed down by a great burden of 'problems'. If an adult is joyful, simple and open, he is not thought of as being wise and deep. This cold philosophy kills off more and more of the good impulses in his nature, so that finally man destroys himself. For this reason, try to become like children, with a heart full of love, always full of life, interested in everything, forgiving others quickly, rejoicing over the smallest of joys, rapidly forgetting all sorrows and failures, always ready to hug the whole world, keeping a heart which does not crystallize into old rigid structures: always with that vital heart that stops you growing old.

Children are full confidence in themselves, they think they are capable of fighting and overthrowing giants because they imagine that they are stronger. When they try and fail, they still go on believing that they can do it! They also believe everything they are told – even the tallest of tall stories – but old people don't believe you, even if you tell them the truth. They are always so very suspicious and say, "My child, I've seen that so many times... I am not so foolish as to believe that sort of thing, you can't pull the wool over my eyes." In fact, you can very easily pull the wool over their eyes, for often they do not see very clearly at all.

I've been asked, "Why do you sometimes behave as merrily as any child?" and my reply is that I feel better that way! Of course I receive less respect that way, but that is no problem for me. Why do people always want esteem and respect? You esteem old people, you respect them, but you don't love them. A mountain is an awe-inspiring sight; you admire it and then you walk on it. A little pearl, on the other hand, you love and want to wear all the time. Do you respect children and bow down to them? No, you caress children (you may sometimes give them a slap also) because the most important thing is that you love them. Love is a warm thing, whereas respect is a fairly chilly affair. Highly placed people, old people and scholars are respected, but it is rare to find them loved. You bow down to a very old man, you make him the profoundest of bows, but you look for the quickest way you can find to get out of his presence.

Those who always want to be respected will lose the love of others. On the other hand, those who want to stay like a child may not be respected, but everyone will love them. If you look only for respect, the day will come when you find yourself very much alone. You will say, "When I walk down the street, I am greeted with much consideration, but I am all alone and no one comes to warm me." Respect never fills our hearts to overflowing... only love is capable of making us happy. So the person who wants to be overwhelmed must choose love and therefore must become like a child.

Love and wisdom, those are the two things we must possess: love in the heart and wisdom in the intellect. The heart must stay eternally young and the intellect must be very, very old. If

"Except ye become as little children" 33

the opposite happens, with the heart growing old and the intellect staying half-baked, the results are disastrous. The man who is always discontented, sad, disappointed, suspicious and uneasy, has the heart of an old man: he is unloving, uninterested, unprogressing, and very often his intellect stays infantile, too. Childhood and age are not bad in themselves but you must know what should be young and what should be old. Occasionally you come across very great scholars of extreme distinction who possess extraordinary youthfulness of heart and that is the ideal; that is perfection. Unfortunately, however, this perfection is only very rarely achieved.

II

Nature, in her intelligence, established that children should stay by their parents for several years as, in order to develop and grow, they need models. Parents are often rather odd models, certainly not always exemplary, and as children instinctively imitate their parents, the results are not going to be marvellous if their parents are not quite up to the mark. For this reason adults, too, need models who surpass them. However, they do not like facing this fact; they do not seek models because they believe that they are already perfect. This attitude is very unfortunate; well-wadded with their own self-satisfied complacency, they walk towards disaster.

Do you realize that I, too, have models so that I can become what I long to be? Yes indeed but, as I haven't found any sufficiently perfect models here on earth, I look for them elsewhere and because of my models I make progress every day. I agree that I only make tiny little steps, but with this minute amount of progress made each day I will have covered an immense amount of ground in several thousands of years. Yes, I have enough patience to work for thousands of years more...!

So then, children come to live closely together with adults so that they can have models, but also so that the adults can have in front of them examples of the children they themselves should become. As it says in the Gospels, only children will enter the Kingdom of God. An adult is too big, too heavy, too serious; but a little laughing, leaping, capering child... of course the gates open straightaway to him! Do you believe that, even with all these explanations, everyone will decide from this day forth to become as little children? No, no, I can assure you that they will go on as before, weighing themselves down with burdens, worries and complications, because they have not understood anything at all.

Look at the child. He has no worries, no job to do; his parents look after him, feed him, wash him and dress him. Adults, on the contrary, are weighed down with the duties and complications of life... they have to earn the money to cover all the needs of their family, to feed them, house them, protect them and so on.... Of course there are cases where children are badly treated, abandoned, thrown out onto the street by their parents, and there are cases where rich and privileged adults pass their lives in happiness and tranquility, but these are the exceptions.

Because he needs protection and because he does not have either enough strength or the necessary faculties to provide for himself and his life, the child must accept the authority and advice of adults. Later on, when he feels strong, capable and intelligent, he will take on responsibilities; he will want to work, to impose his wishes on others, to show his mettle. That, of course, is when his troubles begin: simply because he counts on himself, on his own faculties, his own strength, his own way of seeing things.

Whether you are an adult or a child is, in fact, more a question of attitude than of age. Amongst adults, some hold adult attitudes, whereas others hold the attitudes of a child. You can, of course, look at this question from other aspects but I leave all that to psychologists and moralists. The one thing that really interests me is to know how to lead the spiritual life. Look at disciples and above all, look at Initiates! Instead of handling their lives themselves, organizing it to suit themselves, they abandon themselves completely to the Will of God. They want to stay children, by which I mean they want to stay obedient to their heavenly parents, following

"Except ye become as little children" 37

them and, above all, following their advice. The instant they choose this attitude, Heaven shows its concern for them by nurturing them, watching over them and protecting them.

Many people – imagining that they have become adult – feel strong, free, masters of their own destiny, and so believe that they have no need of a Heavenly Father or a Divine Mother: the connections between them are therefore severed. It is from that very moment that all sorts of disasters start arriving: Heaven no longer bothers with them. Why should it... after all they are adults, aren't they? If only they had gone on being children, by which I mean that, instead of always wanting to proclaim their independence from Heaven, they had allowed themselves to be guided by Heaven; following its advice; trusting it by walking along with their hands in the hands of their heavenly parents, then they would have been looked after and protected always.

You protest that one cannot stay a child all one's life. Of course I realize that, but once again I have to explain that I am not saying that you should keep an infantile mentality but that, even when you are grown-up, you should have the attitude of a child towards Heaven: you should be docile, obedient and full of love. It is quite simply a question of attitude. Heaven will notice a person with this attitude and will not only never abandon him, but will always send help and light. Heaven will not come to your aid unless you are a child. "Even if I am an old man of ninety-nine?" you say. Age has nothing to do with it at all; sublime entities do not look at your wrinkles, your white hair or your birth certificate; they see that you are an adorable child, that your attitude is one of a son or daughter of God and so they bring you to Paradise.

The words of Jesus have not always been well understood nor well interpreted. I can hear the unspoken question, "Good heavens, is he preaching that we should be as weak and ignorant as children?" No, of course not; it is not the faults of children that we should copy, but their qualities of obedience, of trust, which make them listen to their parents, follow them, learning and acting according to their advice.

I have had the opportunity to meet many young people who have such faith in their way of looking at things that they will not accept anyone's advice. Even if it comes from a Master, they will not listen to him. Just to see this kind of mentality means that I can foresee the huge difficulties which lie ahead of them and which they will not be ready to meet or solve correctly. All of this is evident from the simple fact that they have an adult mentality: instead of being like children, aware of their ignorance and weakness, relying on their parents, asking for and following their advice, they rely absolutely on their own opinions. Ah well, these youngsters are already too old and, as a result, they are going to run head on into great problems and great sadness.

If you ask me how long you should continue having this childlike attitude, I would reply: "Until you have become so pure and luminous that the Holy Spirit can come and live in you!" Yes, when the Holy Spirit comes and lives in a man, that man can be considered a true adult. God did not create man to stay a child forever. Both of these periods of childhood and maturity were foreseen by Cosmic Intelligence. First you must be a child for a certain time and then you reach maturity. This maturity is not the same as the majority reached at twenty-one or eighteen; that is legal majority, but it is not the one of which I speak. As I see it, even at ninety-nine most people have not reached their majority because they do not possess spiritual maturity.

It is only when a person has received the Holy Spirit that he becomes truly adult, walking in the light, possessing a guide and clearly seeing the way ahead. These are the only ones recognized as adult by Heaven; all others are just recalcitrant children. Yes, all those who have not yet reached this spiritual maturity are regarded as babies by Heaven. So then, I have made it quite clear that man must not always stay a child but that, until he has received the light – the spirit of God which brings everything – he must maintain a child's approach by always staying obedient, humble and attentive to Heaven. When you see people in the clutches of inextricable difficulties, it is clear proof that they are no more than disobedient children because true adults no longer suffer; they are always in the light. All those, however, who have not wanted to keep this attitude of the child until they reach their spiritual maturity and who have therefore become premature adults, all those people, obviously, are going to suffer.

So then, what to do now? Well, it is very simple. As you have not become adults yet, you must ask to be enlightened and guided by your heavenly parents. When they see that you are becoming stronger and stronger, more radiant, luminous and full of love, they will decide to give you your majority and from then on the spirit of light will never stop illuminating and inspiring you. You will no longer have the same difficulties as all those other so-called adults who think they are living independent lives. I repeat that until you have been recognized as adult

"Except ye become as little children" 41

by Heaven, you must act as a humble obedient child in order to be able to enter the Kingdom of God.

I want to be sure you understand what I am saying. When I say you must be humble and obedient I am speaking of your attitude to God, not toward humans. So often the idea of humility has been taken to mean that one should be obedient and accept submissively anything from anyone, and consequently many people have been obedient towards tyrants, rich, powerful men, and executioners, whereas what I am saying is that you must be faithful, devoted, submissive and obedient towards the divine principle alone.

In fact, even in church amongst members of the clergy you do not see many people who are really adult: they talk from their own point of view according to their own personal inspiration and that is not what should be done. Before a man can preach, the Spirit must take possession of him, because it is the Spirit which must speak through him so that his words are not an expression of himself but the expression of Cosmic Intelligence, words of wisdom and heavenly light. Only when a man no longer talks in his own name is that man an adult. There are Masters who have authority and who impose themselves, but it is not they themselves who impose: it is the Spirit within, and the Spirit has the right to impose itself. However, you must not impose yourself before having received the Spirit as that is very dangerous; you do not have the right to give orders and command others before you reach your majority for, if you do, you are acting as an adult ahead of time.

Spiritual life brings periods of transformation which mark the passage from one stage to another in the same way as the physiological passages of puberty and the menopause. These phases are not quite so noticeably apparent on the spiritual plane, but they are very significant because of the great changes they produce in the inner life. So just as in physical development there is a progression from childhood to adolescence to adulthood, there is a similar progression in our spiritual evolution. You must remain a child as long as you have not reached the maturity of an adult, but once you have become an adult there is no longer any question of continuing to behave like a child.

So now, with all this explanation today, the words of Jesus have become much easier to understand. "Except ye become as little children ye shall not enter into the kingdom of heaven." Yes, the day you stop trusting your Heavenly Father and Divine Mother, loving them, putting yourself entirely into their hands, you will begin to feel the burdens of life in all their misery and ugliness. You will be bored and weary; no longer will you have the gaiety of a joyful, carefree child, singing and dancing and playing; you will become wrinkled and decrepit because you have too much weight on your shoulders. If, however, even though you have all the responsibilities of an adult, and despite all your cares and duties, you still want to remain a heavenly child, confidently persuaded that you have parents on high who love you, then you will smile, then you will blossom, then you will be beautiful and luminous.

Is that quite clear now? We all have to do nothing more than become the children of Heaven; at that moment we will feel the love of our Father and our Mother, their presence, their help and, ceaselessly, we will be supported, protected, encouraged and enlightened. Whereas all those who believe themselves to be so superior that they are able to cut the link with Heaven will feel unhappy and abandoned, alone in the cold and the dark. Many people nowadays who believe that they are very mature, intelligent and powerful are in fact in that state of misery. Those who have left their heavenly parents are weighed down with difficulties and burdens. So then, be like little children, cling like limpets to your Father and Mother and be full of confidence in them. All difficulties are resolved for the one who feels that he is a child of God, for Heaven never lets its children cry all on their own but always comes to their rescue.

3

THE UNJUST STEWARD

"And he said also unto his disciples, There was a certain rich man, which had a steward; and the same was accused unto him that he had wasted his goods. And he called him, and said unto him, How is it that I hear this of thee? Give an account of thy stewardship; for thou mayest no longer be steward. Then the steward said within himself, What shall I do? For my lord taketh away from me the stewardship; I cannot dig; to beg I am ashamed. I am resolved what to do, that, when I am put out of the stewardship, they may receive me into their houses. So he called every one of his lord's debtors unto him, and said unto the first, How much owest thou unto my lord? And he said, An hundred measures of oil. And he said unto him, Take thy bill, and sit down quickly, and write fifty. Then said he to another, And how much owest thou? And he said, An hundred measures of wheat. And he said unto him, Take thy bill, and write fourscore. And the lord commended the unjust steward, because he had done wisely; for the children of this world are in their generation wiser than the children of light. And I say unto you, Make to yourselves friends of the mammon of unrighteousness; that, when ye fail, they may receive you into everlasting habitations. He that is faithful in that which is least is faithful also in much; and he that is unjust in the least is unjust also in much. If, therefore, ye have not been faithful in the unrighteous mammon, who will commit to your trust the true riches? And if ye have not been faithful in that which is another man's, who shall give you that which is your own? No servant can serve two masters: for either he will hate the one, and love the other; or else he will hold to the one and despise the other. Ye cannot serve God and mammon."

St. Luke 16 : 1-13

This is a very difficult parable to interpret and up to now I have never come across any commentaries, whether philosophical or theological which give a true explanation of it.

Jesus speaks of a steward who acts unjustly towards his master and then, surprisingly, he advises us to imitate this man. "I say unto you, Make to yourselves friends of the mammon of unrighteousness"... and then he adds, "He that

The unjust steward

is faithful in that which is least is faithful also in much...", so after first having praised infidelity, Jesus now seems to be praising fidelity. "If therefore ye have not been faithful in the unrighteous mammon, who will commit to your trust the true riches?" Jesus is encouraging fidelity and infidelity at one and the same time and therefore, at first glance, this parable is incomprehensible.

In order to grasp the meaning of this text it is necessary first of all to imagine human beings as they are seen by Initiatic Science, with their two natures, the lower and the higher. These two natures have the same faculties of thinking, feeling and acting but use these faculties in two quite different and opposed directions. From a philosophical point of view you cannot find the exact boundaries between these two natures, because they melt into each other (a little like the colours of the spectrum which you can see very clearly from a distance but, when near, it is impossible to see exactly where one colour changes to the next) – but from a practical point of view in daily life, if you know how to observe, you can distinguish them very clearly from each other.

Before we go any further, let us pause to look at this diagram, it will throw light on this question of man's two natures. Each nature is shown with three divisions which correspond to the three functions in man: his intellect, his heart, his willpower, or, if you prefer, his thoughts, feelings and actions. Each of these functions has a position, a vehicle, a body, through which it can express itself. In the bottom half of the diagram (which represents the lower nature) you will find the physical, astral and mental bodies, and in the higher nature the causal, buddhic and atmic bodies. We could quite easily use other terms. For the lower nature you could say will, heart, intellect; and for the higher nature, higher intellect (or reason), higher heart (or soul) and higher will (or spirit).

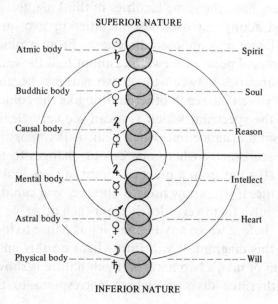

The unjust steward

You may wonder what the three big concentric circles are. They represent the links which exist between the higher and lower bodies. The atmic body, which corresponds to the spirit, and which is force, strength, divine will, is reflected through the physical body, which itself represents strength, will and power on the material plane. The buddhic body, which represents the soul with all its most highly elevated sentiments of love, sacrifice and goodness, is linked to the human heart or the astral body. The causal body, vehicle of the most vast and luminous thoughts, is linked to the intellect or the mental body. These links can explain many obscure situations in life, and also illuminate many passages in sacred books.

Each of these different bodies is placed under the influence of signs of the zodiac and the planets. For example, you can see that on the diagram the physical body is placed under the influences of the Moon and Saturn and the atmic is under those of the Sun and Saturn. The astral and buddhic bodies are influenced by Venus and Mars and the causal bodies by Mercury and Jupiter.

In traditional symbology particular importance is given to those two great lights, the sun and the moon, for our earth in particular is placed under their influence. Sometimes it is the sun which predominates, sometimes the moon. The sun, the moon and the earth represent the threefold division of spirit, soul and body which in turn reflects the three worlds: the divine world, the psychic world, and the physical world. The sun is also the symbol of stability born of reason – the higher nature – whereas the moon is the symbol of trouble, of fermenting passions, of the lower nature. In order to simplify things, I call the higher nature "individuality" and the lower nature "personality" and I will explain why later on.

Personality is represented by the lower half of the diagram and individuality by the upper half. Individuality is manifest in the highest virtues of wisdom on the causal plane, love on the buddhic plane and truth on the atmic plane. Each virtue possesses a particular power: wisdom brings man light, true knowledge based on eternal principles, love gives him the desire to live and gives him happiness, whilst truth brings him freedom. Truth can give man happiness and the taste for life, but only through the intermediary of love. Without love, truth cannot bring happiness: on the contrary, it very often begins by bringing suffering and torment. For this reason many people refuse to see the truth because they fear it. Wisdom can free a man and bring

The unjust steward

him happiness, but only through the intermediary of truth and love. Wisdom cannot free men nor make them happy; on the contrary, it even makes them melancholy and discouraged. As for love, it can neither free nor enlighten; it only brings expansion, joy and life. If, however, you unite love, wisdom and truth, you have abundance, all the blessings of Heaven and total perfection of being.

Unfortunately, the majority of people think they can find liberty, happiness and light in the expression of their lower nature, whereas with the personality one only finds slavery on the physical plane, grief, sorrow, vexation, afflictions on the astral, emotional plane, and mistakes and errors on the mental plane. Despite its seductive appearance, this is all that the human personality can give.

So many people waste their lives trying to content their own personality or that of others.... The mother spends her time satisfying the caprices of her child, the husband those of his wife, and the wife those of her husband... and where does it get them? Personality, ungrateful in its very nature, immediately forgets all the good that has ever been shown it and instead of gratitude retaliates with indifference, disdain or even hatred. Those who satisfy only the lower nature of others will never be rewarded. They should realize this and then they would not be tempted to complain when the roof falls in on them. Before making sacrifices for others, people should ask themselves whether it is the higher or the lower nature they are serving.

If you do not want to be disappointed by people, feed their souls, feed their spirits! Enlighten them, direct them to the fountainhead, to God Himself, so that they can unite with Him, praise Him and glorify Him. People are constantly amazed when they find that the misplaced faith and confidence which they put in others has been betrayed. Quite simply, it is because they have fed the lower nature. You often hear parents giving their children advice which is aimed uniquely at satisfying the child's personality: they are taught to use stratagems of deceit, to long for money and pleasure and to aim for their own personal good, regardless of whether it is to the detriment of others. As they grow up, these well instructed children start putting this advice into practice; they begin to act in their own interests against those of their parents who, of course, react with loud complaints. Really honest parents would realize that it was they themselves who were responsible for this sorry state of affairs.

People appreciate you doing something for

The unjust steward

their physical bodies; they like what you do for their material satisfaction, whereas Heaven appreciates only what you do for their souls, their spirits. Nothing will remain of the food which you have given to your friends if you have not added those other ingredients of love, light and freedom. We must change the present way of thinking about kindness, because there are two kinds: one which produces no effects, as it is very quickly wiped out and forgotten, and another whose effects are long lasting. Ordinary people do not know how to feed the spirits of those around them, they do not know how to make them stronger or more beautiful: but true kindness, the real lovingkindness of Initiates, consists in reinstating man once again in the kingdom of his spirit.

It sometimes happens that a Master deals with the personality of his disciples (that is, he heals them or gives them some material help), but he does it always as a secondary action. Very often ordinary kindness develops the worst faults in people as it encourages laziness, increases exploitation of others, augments their belief in the credulity and naïvety of kind people so that instead of being useful, free, independent and capable of dealing with situations in their own right, they become nothing more than parasites on society.

What I have just said to you about personality does not mean that you should kill it, wipe it out, annihilate it. Not at all. It must be the servant of individuality for, without the personality, individuality cannot manifest itself. The personality can be compared to the form of something and the individuality to its contents. The form is necessary but it must express the contents. If the form is stupid and deprived of sense, the subjection of the human being is complete.

The human spirit can do miracles when personality becomes its servant. You must realize that it is the personality which hinders the spirit, stopping it from understanding, creating or acting freely. Look at the people around you and you will notice that the more the personality predominates, the more the person is narrow-minded and limited. So the slightest suggestion of foregone conclusions in philosophical or religious opinions, in human relationships or work, leads to complications in understanding and action. The greatest holder of foregone conclusions is the personality which is irritable, defensive, vengeful and always changing its point of view. Because all the enterprises of the personality have only a self-interested goal, it is condemned never to see the reality of things. When a Master sees people coming to his school with very developed personalities, he already knows what

The unjust steward

obstacles they will encounter and what difficulties he will have in teaching them. For Masters there is an absolute formula that the more personality is mastered – the more it is limited and dominated – the more one becomes free and strong.

Let us pause for a moment and consider these terms "personality" and "individuality". Nowadays they are used interchangeably; you can say either that a man has a strong personality or a strong individuality and mean just the same thing. You may perhaps find other definitions in the dictionary, but to help you understand what I want to explain to you about the higher and lower natures in man, I will tell you that the term personality comes from the latin word "persona". The mask which the actor puts on when he is acting a role in the theatre is his "persona" for, as you are aware, in the days of classical theatre the actors wore masks. So then imagine an actor: one day he plays the role of a reasonable and wise man, the next that of a criminal, a traitor or a seducer. One after another he plays out the roles of Cyrano de Bergerac, Harpagon, Alexander Borgia, St. Louis. All these differing roles represent the personality, always changing, always ephemeral, whereas individuality is represented by the artist who stays constant throughout all these roles.

This example of the actor shows us that personality is mortal, perishable. Like the role which is finished when the production is over, personality only lasts an incarnation. In the next incarnation another personality appears. However, whilst all these changes are going on with the personality, the individuality is not affected, it stays the same, even though it progresses over millennia by accumulating all these experiences lived by all its various personalities. Individuality is manifested in first one role, then another role, dressed in a different personality for each incarnation.

All this is very simple, allowing us to understand that the person who is handsome and in good health in this life will come back poor, sickly and ugly if he makes no spiritual efforts. Whereas the man who works on his spirit, on his divine intelligence or his soul (all the while playing the role which this incarnation imposes on him) acquires qualities, virtues and riches which will remain in his individuality, belonging to him eternally. When he finishes playing the role of this personality, he will depart with all his spiritual luggage and he will then travel throughout the universe with this true wealth. Nothing can take it away from him. Just as the actor who

The unjust steward

has gained much from his roles, learnt to improve himself, grown a little, leaves the stage with nobler, more profound ideas, so should man leave this earthly stage enriched by his experience.

What happens to the goods of the man who has used his life only to accumulate material riches? On leaving his earthly role he is forced to abandon them – that is the law – and then very quickly he finds that he is poor, stripped of everything. His individuality, which also leaves without any luggage, without any spiritual acquisitions, comes back on earth poor and naked and so has to incarnate in a personality deprived of all benefits, since it did not deserve them. This person then has to start working enormously hard to acquire wealth, a job, a home and so on.

I am not saying that you should not possess material things, clothes and houses, not at all. But just as the decor and costumes are indispensable to the actors, so all these things are necessary on earth: they are no more than that.

You are now sufficiently prepared to understand the meaning of the parable of the unjust steward.

The personality and the individuality have their place in the great world, the 'macrocosm', and also in the little world, in the 'microcosm' of man. In man, the seat of the personality is the stomach and everything which is found below the diaphragm; whereas the seat of the individuality is found in the lungs, in the heart and brain, in everything which is above the diaphragm. The horizontal line in the diagram which I have given you corresponds to the diaphragm.

Perhaps you think that everything situated below the diaphragm has no thoughts, feelings and activity. Don't you believe it! The stomach has a brain, a heart and a will. We even say of some people that their heart is in their stomach. I have no intention of creating a new anatomy, but you must know that these two regions – above and below the diaphragm – represent the two masters in the house of man, two masters requiring service. Yes indeed, it is quite a story!

When man comes on earth, he enters the service of a master: he serves the physical body with its instincts, but sooner or later he is dismissed from his job, or in other words, he dies. If he is intelligent, he will think as the steward does in the parable. "What shall I do? for my lord taketh away from me the stewardship; I cannot dig; to beg I am ashamed". The reasonable steward knows very well that when he leaves this physical body – his eternally discontented master – that he will want to go on working on earth

The unjust steward

but he will no longer have the means. As he still has the same desires for eating and drinking and experiencing all sorts of pleasures, even though he has left the physical plane for the astral plane, he will be tempted to beg, by coming down near living people and trying to satisfy his desires through their activities. That is what happens to stewards who have been very faithful towards the personality: once they get to the other side, they become beggars on the astral plane and they gather in all the unhealthy spots where crowds go for amusement so that they too can take part in their pleasures.

So you see the unfaithful steward in Jesus' parable was intelligent as he did not want to be placed in this category of begging spirits. Guided by his reason, he decided to make friends with the help of unrighteous mammon, to reduce the debt owed by his master's debtors. This means that instead of giving his stomach copious meals and his other organs excessive pleasures as most people normally do, he diminished the proportion of food or satisfaction which he thought he owed to each of them. In other words, he established a diet of restrictions for the personality. He diminished the number of copious meals, glasses of alcohol, cigars, mistresses, as well as the energies, thoughts and time which should have been given to be swallowed up by his insatiable master, and gave them secretly to invisible friends in the eternal tabernacles on high. He made economies, saved up some capital, which he then put into a heavenly bank, so that he would be recognized and welcomed whenever he went to draw money. He consecrated time and energy, he gave some of his love, his thoughts and his feelings to his individuality, instead of saving them all for his personality. He was unfaithful to his personality in order to win new friends with the riches he had "unjustly" collected.

If we do not interpret the parable in this way, we will never be able to understand just why the steward was praised by his master. Who was the master who praised him? It certainly was not the personality; since it had been harmed, it would not be the one to congratulate him! It was the individuality which said, "You are very intelligent and you have done well." There is only one infidelity, one injustice permissable and that is towards the personality, that is to say towards all that is inferior and perishable in oneself. We have no right to be unfaithful towards God, angels, purity and goodness. But everyone behaves in quite the opposite way; they are faithful to their stomachs, sex and personality whilst being unfaithful to God. They bustle busily about occupying themselves with anything to do with

The unjust steward

their passions and their lower desires, but they betray the Lord ceaselessly. Think how many people are faithful to the patron of their local bistro: they go to see him every day! Others are faithful to their tobacco or to a particular sort of passion, to a vice or an unhealthy habit. Very few people are faithful to higher habits. True fidelity means never forgetting to pray, to study, to meditate, to do all the spiritual exercises.

You may be wondering what the significance is of the debtors who had their debts reduced and what was the nature of those debts. The debtors are entities in the invisible world; they come to take certain spiritual elements from man and have to repay him in energies, in less subtle forces. When man pays back what he owes to these entities, he renounces the forces which they would have given him, that is to say he takes the path of abstinence, he practises fasting, chastity, silence, prayer and meditation. This restriction means that the body does not require the usual high expenditure of energy. It must be realized that when the physical body gives up some of its desires it means that the higher self can grow stronger, because it is freed from having to provide so many forces and fluids. Whereas if the lower side devotes itself to eating and amusement, the higher side cannot manifest and it grows weaker: for it is the higher self which provides all the energies which are manifested on the physical plane.

You will have noticed, however, that Jesus did not say in the parable that the unjust steward should give back all of the debtors' debts, but merely a part. This means that you should not practice excessive restrictions, that you should not go to extremes of mortification of the flesh and total asceticism. Jesus showed quite clearly that man should work for the first master (individuality), but that he did not have the right to leave the second master (personality) by depriving himself of everything and risking death through such extreme renunciation. He must be unfaithful to the second master, but only to a certain extent.

Let us take the example of a woman who is only interested in her physical appearance. She entirely neglects her intellectual and spiritual development in her preoccupation with her face and body. She does, indeed, become extremely seductive, sweet as honey, attracting wasps and flies from afar. She has numerous lovers and everywhere she goes she is fêted... but a few years later her looks start fading and her friends leave her. This is perfectly normal. People seek out only those who can give them something and a woman is left with nothing once her beauty has gone. If this woman had acted like the unjust but

The unjust steward

sensible steward, if she had seen that one day her master would dismiss her, she would have prepared for such a change of situation; she would have started to study, to develop goodness and intelligence so that when she no longer had any beauty, she could still keep her friends. Then she would have kept them because she would have stayed lovely and a delight to look at, despite her age! I have often noticed that when women cultivate their individuality, the older they grow, the more radiant, charming, luminous they become. As for the others, the less said about them the better!

Since each one of us will inevitably come to that moment when we will be dismissed by our master, we must prepare ourselves for that moment and therefore create friends on another plane. These friends are not on the physical plane. The phrase in the parable is symbolic, "And I say unto you, Make to yourselves friends of the mammon of unrighteousness". The way to make these friends is to reduce the amount you give yourself. If you think, or have thought up to now, that you owe your master, the stomach, five dozen oysters, a kilo of caviar, a dozen sausages, several turkeys... all washed down liberally with the best wine followed by several liqueurs and cigars, try to cut down this menu a little! Not only will you be much better fed, but you will also have freed certain entities from having to provide the necessary energies to digest such a meal. In this way you will make friends of these invisible beings, and later on they will receive you gladly in the eternal tabernacles.

This restriction of joys and pleasures on the physical plane should also be paralleled on the astral and mental planes for, as you saw on the diagram, all these three planes belong to the personality. Jesus said, "He that is faithful in that which is least, is faithful also in much; and he that is unjust in the least is unjust also in much. If therefore ye have not been faithful in the unrighteous mammon, who will commit to your trust the true riches?" and this means that if you are not faithful to the individuality in little earthly things, you will not be given the great riches of the spirit.

You say, "Fine, fine, we have understood that we must nourish the individuality and that we must not let the personality die of starvation either, but how are we to know exactly how much we should give to each master?" My answer is to remind you of the scene in the Gospels where the Pharisees ask Jesus a question about taxes for Caesar, hoping that his reply would give them grounds for accusation: "Should we

The unjust steward

pay taxes to Caesar?" But Jesus perceived their wickedness (for he could read their thoughts), and said, "Show me the tribute money." "And they brought unto him a penny. And he said unto them, Whose is this image and superscription? They say unto him, Caesar's. Then saith he unto them, Render therefore unto Caesar the things which are Caesar's and unto God the things that are God's." Who is Caesar? Caesar is none other than one of the forms of personality. Yes, we all have a Caesar in us who is making constant demands. He must be given something so that he can live, but not everything. You ask, "But how much, precisely, should be given to Caesar?"

To make it quite clear to you, I will use yet another image. When you burn a piece of wood, say perhaps a branch of a tree, what do you see? First of all you see flames and more flames which blaze forth, then there is gas, but less than the flames, then even less water vapour and then, finally, you are left with a mere handful of ashes. Where have all these elements gone? The fire, the gas, the vapours all went up to Heaven, whereas only the ash remains. In that fact lies a clear indication of what you should give the personality: one quarter belongs to the earth and should go to the personality, and the other three quarters belong to the individuality. Yes, one quarter is quite enough for the personality; it needs looking after, needs to be fed a little so that it does not die, but all the rest must be given to the individuality.

Jesus explained many things to his disciples, but the Evangelists only wrote down a very small part of these explanations, and so, when we now try to interpret his words, it is not at all easy. Of course there is always the possibility of interpretation by poring over each word; comparing all the different versions, going back to the original Hebrew and early Greek; looking for omissions, deliberate mistakes, clerical errors; or approaching the problem from the historical point of view. This approach is known as biblical exegesis. Many fling themselves enthusiastically into this type of research but I say that if you continued until eternity in this way you would never find the key to the Scriptures. What interests me is not how the Holy Books were written, what faults in translation or errors in transcription there are; what interests me is knowing what Jesus had in his head, in his very soul at the moment when he was using those parables and that is very difficult to discover by exegesis. The words of Jesus are still living in the archives of the universe, the Akasha Chronica, and it is to there we have to raise ourselves if we are to

The unjust steward

find the meaning. Once we have understood it, we can then go back to the text and interpret it.

If we use the ordinary intellect we cannot go beyond the level of form. Truth however is not found at this level; it can only be found by going very high. True meaning lives on the higher planes and, if we do not interpret Holy Books by raising ourselves up to this level, we will not be able to get to the heart of the meaning. The first method of exegesis, that of using the intellect alone, is the personality's method; the second, of rising up within yourself, is that of the individuality. Using the method of individuality, the spirit has access to very highly elevated regions where the explanations for everything lie, whereas the method of the personality makes us go down to a level where there are no more than scraps and deformed fragments of the truth. Great discussions and erudite arguments only distance us from both meaning and content: they become more and more ungraspable.

Jesus finishes the parable by speaking of two masters. "No servant can serve two masters: for either he will hate the one and love the other; or else he will hold to the one and despise the other. Ye cannot serve God and mammon." By this he meant that you cannot serve both your higher and lower natures at the same time. The text goes on to say, "That which is highly esteemed among men is abomination in the sight of God". Therefore, that which is glorious for the world, for the personality, is odious to the individuality, to the spirit. Personality is always on the lookout for public approval, regardless of how ignorant the mob may be; whereas the individuality longs only for the approval of the divine world.

However, I have said before and I say again that you must not kill your personality. Personality is magnificent when it is subservient to the orders of the individuality. We could do nothing here on earth without the personality, but when it takes over the role of mistress of the house it can give only bad advice.

4

"LAY UP FOR YOURSELVES TREASURES IN HEAVEN"

"Lay not up for yourselves treasures upon earth, where moth and rust doth corrupt, and where thieves break through and steal: but lay up for yourselves treasures in heaven, where neither moth nor rust doth corrupt and where thieves do not break through nor steal.... No man can serve two masters; for either he will hate the one and love the other or else he will hold to the one and despise the other. Ye cannot serve God and mammon."

St. Matthew 6 : 19-20, 24

This passage from the Gospel according to St. Matthew should be looked at in conjunction with the sixteenth chapter of St. Luke's Gospel on the unjust steward. First of all each passage deals, in an identical fashion, with the question of riches and then both continue with a comment on two masters. "No man can serve two masters; for either he will hate the one and love the other or else he will hold to the one and despise the other. Ye cannot serve God and mammon."

"Lay not up for yourselves treasures upon earth, where moth and rust doth corrupt and where thieves break through and steal: but lay up for yourselves treasures in heaven...." There are two very different sorts of banks in Jesus' mind; the banks of earth and the banks of Heaven, each with very different employees. Man himself represents these two banks and they both function simultaneously in a common building, in his inner self. These two banks are only branch establishments of the two great cosmic banks which supply them.

Are you surprised that I should use such a comparison to interpret the Gospels? I do it precisely because the life of our visible world is modelled on invisible realities. "That which is below is a reflection of that which is above": I use the word reflection advisedly because the beauty and light of the invisible world can never be found on earth. There do, however, exist correspondences which allow comparisons between the two worlds and which help us to understand that which is in the world above thanks to what we see here in the world below, in our world. What then are these two banks of Heaven and earth? They are our old friends personality

"Lay up for yourselves treasures in heaven" 75

and individuality of whom I have talked many times before.

Banks usually provide three different types of service. Firstly, you can deposit your money or place valuables in strongboxes where they will be safe. The second service deals with the transfer of capital and with loans. The third activity deals with financial transactions and with stock market operations. These three services can be found in the structure of the personality. The strongboxes correspond to the physical body's reserves; the transfer of capital corresponds to the feelings, to the astral plane, to the world of the heart which is constantly establishing relations based on interest. The financial operations correspond to the mental plane, to the intellect, which thinks of nothing but making calculations at others' expense, always imagining what advantages can be gained from their present or future ruin. This earthly bank always gets richer at others' expense and yet all the time it tries to convince everyone that all it does, thinks and feels is entirely inspired by love and respect for its neighbours.

I said to you just now that each word Jesus uses is full of meaning. So we will now see what is meant by, "Lay up for yourselves treasures in heaven, where neither worm* nor rust doth corrupt and where thieves do not break through nor steal", by looking at the three words of "rust", "worm" and "thieves".

Let us begin with rust. Alchemists looked for the philosopher's stone, it is said, so that they could transform metals into gold. Why gold? Of all metals, gold is the only one to be rust-free, uncorrodible by water, air or acid; it is soluble only in "royal water", a mixture of nitric acid and hydrochloric acid. Iron, on the hand, when in contact with humid air, rusts very quickly and so is destroyed little by little. So we can see rust as a symbol of that which attacks metal and, speaking generally, the mineral kingdom. If we are to look at the mineral kingdom in the hierarchy of the natural kingdoms we could say it corresponds to the physical plane; and so rust is symbolic of that which destroys the physical plane, the human body.

When we consider worms or moths we are moving into the astral world, the world of the heart and of feelings. Anyone whose heart is filled with hate, doubt, pride, contempt and violence is the prey of worms. Do we not talk about someone who is *consumed* with hate? If you cut

---

* The French versions of this biblical quotation frequently give *worm* rather than *moth*.

"Lay up for yourselves treasures in heaven" 77

a worm in pieces thinking in this way to destroy it, you will find that in fact it multiplies itself. This is a very significant phenomenon from the symbolic point of view: remember the mythical combat of Hercules with the hydra of Lerna. The hydra was a monstrous serpent with seven heads which sprouted again as quickly as they were cut off. The only way to conquer the hydra was by cutting off the seven heads simultaneously. Hercules in fact triumphed over the hydra by using fire. As the hydra represents the seven deadly sins which are reborn as fast as one tries to destroy them, the only way to success is to use the sacred fire of love which burns all the heads at once. The point I wish to make here is that in speaking of worms Jesus wanted to draw our attention to those enemies which attack us on the astral plane, those desires which consume us.

The mention of thieves is again symbolic. The robber arrives armed with false keys, a dagger, a revolver, and he waits for night to fall so that he can start his work. When all is dark and men are sleeping, he creeps into the house. Robbers are symbols of our enemies on the mental plane, for the man whose intellect is darkened or drowsy will be attacked by thieves; wherever darkness is, robbers come. These robbers are invisible entities, lurking doubts and worries. All these thoughts leave you stripped, weak, exhausted, which is proof enough that robbers have entered and taken away your valuables. If you cannot show me your treasures of strength, joy and peace it is quite clear to me that the robbers have been to visit you. Robbers are thoughts which have worked away in the darkness to take away your inspiration and your faith....

The rust, moths and robbers of which Jesus spoke act on different planes; on the physical, astral and mental planes. We can place them on

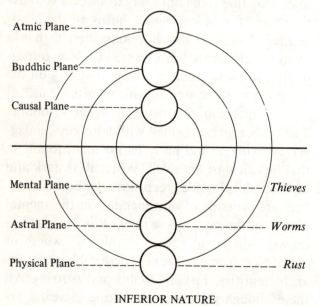

"Lay up for yourselves treasures in heaven" 79

the diagram which we studied in a previous lecture.

One day, an iron bar covered with rust looked at a plough when it was brought back from the fields to the farm and asked it why it was so shining. "I shine because I work", replied the plough, "You live in idleness and so you are covered with rust." The lazy man's willpower is attacked by rust; the heart of the sensual man is eaten up by moths; and the darkened intellect is visited, fatally, by robbers. Jesus put us on our guard against these three categories of enemy by saying, "Lay not up for yourselves treasures upon earth". Look what happens to the man who limits himself to earthly treasures... it is no longer necessary for him to walk as he has a car; he no longer writes as he has secretaries who do it for him; he no longer talks as others talk for him; and he no longer thinks as others think for him... there is nothing left for him to do but to eat, drink, sleep and keep mistresses! Slowly but surely he gets buried deeper in inertia, passions and darkness; he has laid up treasures in a bank but sooner or later they will be attacked by rust, moths and robbers.

Later on Jesus himself explains, "For where your treasure is, there will your heart be also." This is something you need to know, for everything changes on earth... you are not going to keep your houses, factories or cars eternally, nor your wife who, perhaps, has lovers (nor your husband who, perhaps, has mistresses), nor your children who often turn against their parents. If your heart is in your safe and the safe is ransacked, your heart will be broken. So when Jesus said, "Lay not up for yourselves treasures upon earth... but lay up for yourselves treasures in heaven", he meant, "Detach yourself from the three lower principles of your personality and link yourself to the three higher principles of your individuality, then you will never have to fear rust, moths nor robbers."

Let us look at the picture of a tree. You could say that, diagramatically, it is made of two cones: the cone of the branches with the point at the top and the cone of the roots with the point at the bottom.

The cone pointing upwards is the symbol of spiritual ascension, whereas the upside down cone is the symbol of limitation. The person who goes very low down in his consciousness has neither warmth, nor light, nor movement. He is therefore down amongst the roots of the tree, working with the three lower bodies: physical, astral and mental. Movement, warmth and light only manifest up above in the leaves, flowers and fruit. Those who grow in wisdom, love

"Lay up for yourselves treasures in heaven"   81

and truth live in their three higher bodies – amongst the leaves, flowers and fruit. The roots below prepare the food for the fruit which ripens at the top of the being. The astrological signs placed on the diagram underline the exactitude of the correspondences: at the bottom is the Moon (linked to lower Saturn), sign of laziness. At the top of the diagram is the Sun (linked to higher Saturn), sign of activity.

"Lay up for yourselves treasures in heaven, where neither moth nor rust doth corrupt and

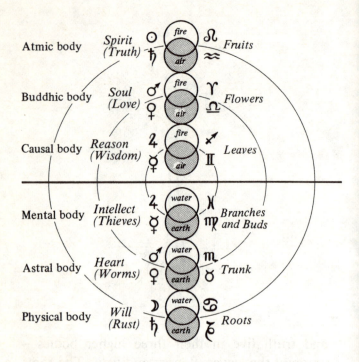

where thieves do not break through nor steal." Now you understand that these treasures can only be acquired by the work of the will, the heart and the intellect as it is activity which prevents rust from corroding; it is love which kills the moths; and it is wisdom which protects you from thieves.

In another passage in the Gospels Jesus said,

"Lay up for yourselves treasures in heaven"

"Ask and it shall be given you; seek and ye shall find; knock and it shall be opened unto you." Once again, these words cannot be explained without acknowledging the trinity of intellect, heart and will in man. Jesus says, "Ask and it shall be given you"; but what are we to ask for and what part of us does the asking? What are we to seek for and with what? What are we to knock on and with what? Ask yourself whether it is the intellect, heart or will that makes demands in you. In fact the intellect does not know how to ask, nor does the will; it is always the heart which asks, whereas the intellect seeks and the will knocks. As the intellect is the seeker, we may ask what it is looking for. Light and wisdom are indispensable if the intellect is to find anything and so that is what it seeks. As for the heart, it asks for warmth and love; to love and be loved. The will knocks to open the doors of its prison so that it can have the freedom to act.

So now everything is quite clear; the intellect seeks wisdom, the heart asks for love, and the will knocks so that it may be free and may create. Unfortunately, however, the majority of mankind uses its intellect, not in looking for wisdom but rather for money and power; the heart asks not for love but pleasure; and the will uses its liberty to destroy rather than to create. Doors open when the will is active, it is true, but the doors are those of prisons, hospitals and cemeteries.

Divine love must be the heart's ideal; the intellect must seek divine wisdom and the will must find divine power. These are the treasures we must lay up for ourselves in Heaven. One day the people who realize this ideal will be able to say, "Do not ask and you will be given, do not seek and you shall find, do not knock and it will be opened unto you." The true child of God no longer needs to ask, seek or knock: Heaven knows what is necessary and gives it to him at exactly the right moment.

5

THE STRAIT GATE

You are beginning to see now that if many passages in the Gospels are still obscure in their meaning it is because people have never learnt how to interpret them in the light of initiatic knowledge. This science teaches us about the structure of man, about the existence and roles of all his different bodies of which materialist scientists are as yet unaware.

Today let us consider the words of Jesus, "It is easier for a camel to go through the eye of a needle than for a rich man to enter into the kingdom of God." The majority of commentators have explained these astonishing words by saying that Jesus used this striking image to underline the impossibility of a rich man (shown here as hard and egotistic) ever being admitted to the Kingdom of God. They did not take the image of the camel at all seriously as it seemed to them to be so wildly exaggerated. In fact it is not at all exaggerated and you will soon understand why.

We have already seen that the astral body in man is the seat of all his feelings, desires, emotions and passions. Greed, cupidity, the desire to possess, to satisfy oneself, are all manifestations of the astral body and if this body is not controlled and taught how to behave, it puffs up more and more, becoming like a monstrous tumour in man. This is what happens with the rich man. In his desire to amass money, land and property he ends up by building himself a gigantic astral body which makes it quite impossible for him to get through the gate of the Kingdom of God. In the Kingdom of God they only let in those who have learnt sacrifice, renunciation and abnegation.

Let us now study the nature of the camel. He knows how to adapt himself perfectly to the life he leads. Hardly anything grows in the desert yet the little he finds is sufficient for him. He can keep on walking for days and nights without needing to stop for food or water. He has, therefore, a miniscule astral body and that is why he symbolizes the Initiate who is content with very little and is able to keep going without flagging throughout the most difficult conditions of life. When Jesus said that the camel could pass through the eye of a needle he did not mean that the camel's physical body could do so, but that his astral body could pass through. Now you can

The strait gate

see how very clear this image is and can understand why I said to you that if you do not know the structure of man, you will never know how to interpret certain passages in the Gospels.

The astral body, that seat of all feeling and passion, begins to manifest in people at the beginning of puberty. Before this period it is the etheric body which is most active. Of course both the astral and mental bodies are alive and, to a certain extent, active; the child experiences strong feelings and understands what is explained to him but his astral body is not really formed until he is about fourteen and the mental body is not formed until he is about twenty-one. The etheric body, which looks after the growth and proper development of the physical body, is most active between birth and seven years of age.

The etheric body acts in the same way in a child as it does in plants. Plants do not possess an astral body because they do not have a true sensitivity or, to be more exact, they have a lesser sensitivity than those of animals or men in that when you cut them, they do not suffer. Plants, then, do not have a developed astral body but they do possess a very powerful etheric body and that is why they never stop growing and developing. If you cut their branches or their stems they grow again and, should you put compost around their roots, they will absorb and transform it into flowers and fruit. Their etheric body purifies everything.

Children are like plants, everything is constantly transformed and purified in them by their etheric bodies whose activity is as yet unhampered by the manifestations of their astral bodies. At about the age of fourteen, adolescence begins and that is when things begin to get complicated. The astral body as it awakens releases all sorts of passionate manifestations: sexuality, aggression and greed. As all these manifestations produce impurities and, consequently, waste products, the etheric body.has to work constantly at eliminating them.

The purity of children, their innocence and candour, come from the fact that their astral bodies have not yet developed. This is another explanation of the words of Jesus, "Except ye become as little children ye shall not enter into the kingdom of heaven". The child will be able to enter the Kingdom of God because he has not got an astral body grown unwieldy from desires, a puffy swollen body which would prevent him from entering. I have already told you that the camel is a symbol and here the child is also a symbol. Jesus did not want to prevent people from becoming adult, but he did encourage them to dominate their astral bodies as their desires

The strait gate

and demands would shut them off from entering the Kingdom of God, that state of consciousness which is all peace, harmony and light. Clearly, the astral body is necessary: if Cosmic Intelligence created man with an astral body it is because it has a role to play. Without it, man would feel nothing, he would have no desires, no feelings and he would be lacking something. However, he must not allow it to develop disproportionately.

Let us return to the text, "It is easier for a camel to go through the eye of a needle than for a rich man to enter into the kingdom of God." Access to the Kingdom of God is indeed difficult because you have to enter by the strait gate which Jesus spoke of elsewhere, "Enter ye in at the strait gate: for wide is the gate, and broad is the way, that leadeth to destruction, and many there be which go in thereat." This strait gate which allows access to the Kingdom of God is none other than the gate of Initiation. Initiation is a discipline, a willed and heroic privation which teaches man how to get rid of his weaknesses and all his negative tendencies. It can be compared to the narrow hole through which the snake has to crawl to shed his skin. A disciple is one who is preparing himself to pass through that strait gate which will remove his old skin or, in other words, his mistaken ideas. Each one of you is called on to pass through this gate. Do not let the thought of that worry you or fill you with fear, but rejoice that it is precisely that passage that will enable you to become a new being filled with new thoughts, feelings and behaviour.

We could say that man passes through three gates in his lifetime; the gates of birth, death and Initiation. All human beings, whether good or bad, pass through the gate of birth. All, without exception, pass through the gate of death, regardless of their quality. The gate of Initiation, however, is open only to those who are capable of great sacrifice and renunciation.

6

"LET HIM WHICH IS ON THE HOUSETOP NOT COME DOWN…"

"When ye therefore shall see the abomination of desolation, spoken of by Daniel the prophet, stand in the holy place (whoso readeth, let him understand): Then let them which be in Judaea flee into the mountains. Let him which is on the housetop not come down to take any thing out of his house: Neither let him which is in the field return back to take his clothes. And woe unto them that are with child, and to them that give suck in those days! But pray ye that your flight be not in the winter, neither on the sabbath day: For then shall be great tribulation, such as was not since the beginning of the world to this time, no, nor ever shall be. And except those days should be shortened, there should no flesh be saved: but for the elect's sake those days shall be shortened. Then if any man shall say unto you, Lo here is Christ, or there; believe it not. For there shall arise false Christs and false prophets, and shall shew great signs and wonders; insomuch that, if it were possible, they shall deceive the very elect. Behold, I have told you before. Wherefore if they shall say unto you, Behold, he is in the desert; go not forth: behold, he is in the secret chambers; believe it not. For as the lightning cometh out of the east and shineth even unto the west, so shall also the coming of the Son of man be. For wheresoever the carcass is, there will the eagles be gathered together. Immediately after the tribulation of those days shall the sun be darkened, and the moon shall not give her light, and the stars shall fall from heaven and the powers of the heavens shall be shaken: And then shall appear the sign of the Son of man in heaven: and then shall all the tribes of the earth mourn, and they shall see the Son of man coming in the clouds of heaven with power and great glory."

St. Matthew 24 : 15-30

Today I am not going to interpret all the predictions which are in the passage I have just read to you as there would be far too many things to explain. However, let us dwell for a moment on the passage where Jesus says, "Immediately after the tribulation of those days shall the sun be darkened, and the moon shall not give her light and the stars shall fall from heaven." Astronomers of course will tell you that this is not possible and they are quite right: the sun, moon and stars of which Jesus is speaking here are symbolic and must be seen as such.

"The sun shall be darkened". The sun represents the human intellect which, in distancing itself from the true Initiatic Science, has constructed a philosophy based on mistaken points of view. Humanity will be forced to abandon this philosophy.

"The moon shall not give her light". The moon represents the domain of feelings and of religion and it will lose its light. This means that official religion, established on false foundations and full of superstition and prejudice will lose its influence.

"The stars shall fall from heaven". All those who occupy a rank or a position of unmerited glory will fall from their pedestals. You see there are a lot of symbols to interpret in this passage.

I could also say much about the warnings given against the false Messiahs who are likely to appear. Indeed, there have been many throughout history who have been tempted to masquerade as the Christ. However, you must not have any doubts that the spirit of Christ will be manifest through those who have fulfilled the conditions necessary to receive him by living a truly spiritual life. If you think that all the great Masters and Initiates are impostors, with the exception of Jesus, you are making a very grave mistake.

Today I will content myself by studying a verse which has often been neglected. Jesus announces these tribulations and then says, "Let him which is on the housetop *not* come down to take anything out of his house". Why should he not go down into his house? Is one safer on the roof of the house during a storm or when bombs are falling during a war? Of course not! Once again, we are dealing with symbols and so we shall now see how to interpret this one of the roof of the house.

Look at this diagram which can be seen as looking roughly like a house.

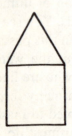

It is made up of a square and a triangle put together. In the language of symbols, the triangle represents the spirit, and the square represents matter. Three is the number of the three divine principles – light, heat, and life; whereas four is the number of the states of matter, found in the solid, the liquid, the gaseous and the igneous. Therefore, when Jesus said, "Let him which is on the housetop not come down", he was imply-

"Let him which is on the housetop..."

ing that in moments of sorrow and tribulation man should not descend into matter to take shelter there, but should stay at a high level in the realm of the spirit.

Let us look at this diagram of the house in three dimensions.

Then let us unfold all the sides first of the body of the house and then of the roof.

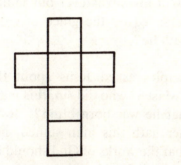

You will notice that this unfolding of these two structures gives us two different crosses: the first is called the Latin cross and the second, the Maltese cross. You are no doubt aware how the pyramids in Egypt are constructed. They have a cubic base buried in the earth which is surmounted by a roof with four triangular faces –the pyramid proper. One of these crosses is therefore under the earth and the other above it. It is not at all by chance that the great Initiates of Egypt chose the form of the pyramid.

The triangle and the square represent spirit and matter. The triangle (3) also symbolizes mercy and love whilst the square (4) symbolizes justice. So we can see that love is placed above justice which serves as its base. According to the law of justice we have to give an account for each and every one of our acts. However, according to the law of love, whatever our faults, we can always be saved by the grace of God. Where does the truth lie?

When the disciples asked Jesus about the man born blind, "Master, who did sin, this man, or his parents, that he was born blind?" Jesus answered, "Neither hath this man sinned, nor his parents; but that the works of God should be made manifest in him." Jesus' reply reveals yet another aspect of the question. There are cases where we do not know why someone suffers or is infirm. Perhaps he has sacrificed himself for another? We do not know. Instead of allowing ourselves to leap to the conclusion that he is a culprit who has to expiate the faults of another earlier life, we should be very careful to refrain from making judgements if we do not know with

"Let him which is on the housetop..."

certainty whether he has committed a crime, or if he has offered to sacrifice himself for some reason which we do not know.

It is very difficult both to reconcile justice and mercy and to understand how each of these qualities manifests itself. In fact no man is worthy of being saved, not even the best of men. We are saved only by the grace of God. If we were to be examined in the light of the law of justice alone, we would never be admitted into the Kingdom of God for, in looking at our case histories, the law would always find several debts which we had not yet paid. Justice is completely implacable; it is not at all concerned whether you are the son of a king or if you are an Initiate.

You are wondering when mercy can be manifested if justice is always carried out. In fact, if justice were truly to be carried out, not one single person would be judged worthy of life. Heaven feeds us, it sends us everything necessary, we are beneficiaries living in abundance and yet, instead of being grateful and saying "thank you", we commit faults each and every day. If justice were to be done we would be smashed to smithereens.

Most people (and even some of the greatest theologians) see mercy as an arbitrary manifestation of the Godhead, which takes place according to what suits God but with little regard as to what is owed by each person. Regardless of whether the individual has done good or bad, if God wants to send him His grace, apparently He does so! Grace and justice are seen as incompatible and given the current ideas on them both, it would seem impossible to reconcile them. However, I am going to show you that, in fact, it is possible and you will see how very simple it is.

The secret is hidden in the diagram of the house, this house on whose roof Jesus advises us to remain. Let us go back to the cross obtained by unfolding the cube, the body of the house. It represents matter, the foundation, but also represents limitation, prison and, by extension, justice. The cross formed by the triangular surfaces of the roof is the cross of grace, of the spirit. If one holds on to justice alone, one remains down in the square, and as the square represents the law and limitations, one is imprisoned. However, the new Teaching of Christ is placed above

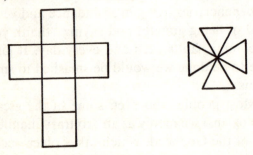

"Let him which is on the housetop..."

justice, and that is why above the cross of justice is found the other cross, the cross of mercy. Justice therefore serves as a basis, a foundation, for grace.

It is interesting to note that many of the crosses which are given as awards of merit have this form ⛌. Unconsciously men work according to the laws of Nature. Each symbol used by a society, each architectual form, corresponds to a certain level of philosophy, showing the evolution of their mentality, knowledge and understanding. If you know how to interpret them, you can determine the tendencies which lie behind all these signs. One day, when we have a little more time, I will explain to you the reasons lying behind the various forms of houses or temples used by different races over the centuries.

Why is the pyramid's base buried in the earth? It is there as an indication that our higher selves – that spiritual trinity of love, wisdom and truth (or if you prefer, faith, hope and love) –want to work and transform our physical bodies, buried in matter. But for that to happen you must understand how spirit, symbolized by 3, becomes 4. 3 is the number of God and 4 is that of incarnation in matter. The virtues of the divine trinity cannot incarnate in man except through the four principles of his heart, mind, soul and spirit. These four principles are symbolized by the roof of the pyramid which has as its support the physical body, the cube, and which work on the body.

Let us return now to the question of justice and mercy. If you want to build a house, you give your builders a blueprint and they set to work. Suppose, however, that a little while later you find you have not got enough money available to finish the work. You have done all the groundwork; the foundations are there, the walls have been built, but the question is how to go on, how the missing roof can be added. You go to the bank and, if it is satisfied that you already have a certain amount of capital, it will agree to make you a loan. Do you understand this? This does not mean to say that the bank will lend money to all comers, but if you have got some capital, some land or some property, it will add what is necessary.

In exactly the same way, mercy is not freely available to all but only to those who have already made preparations, built something, shown that they possess some capital. Mercy observes and then says, "This person is a real worker who meditates, does spiritual exercises and prays. Because the walls of the temple have been built, I will add what is needed for the

"Let him which is on the housetop..."

roof." Mercy goes where the groundwork has been done, where something has already been constructed and prepared; grace is the roof on top of the house, it is the triangle on the square. Therefore the grace of God can go to everyone, to all the world. The only exception is for the lazy. Grace cannot go to those who have not worked, who have begun nothing. It goes to those who have built the foundations of their existence, to those who work on regenerating their beings by eating pure food, thinking pure thoughts and feeling pure feelings. Mercy is therefore a quality higher than justice, but nevertheless it still obeys a certain justice and so in this way mercy is reconciled with justice.

When Jesus says that the man on the roof should not try to go down into his house in order to collect anything he meant that, when he finds himself in difficulties, the man who lives the Teaching of wisdom, love and truth should not descend to the material level to look for help which will be of no use. He should stay up on the roof, up there in his spirit, because it is only there that he will be in absolute safety. And it is only at this level, too, that mercy is to be found.

7

THE CALMING OF THE STORM

"And the same day, when the even was come, he saith unto them, Let us pass over unto the other side. And when they had sent away the multitude, they took him even as he was in the ship. And there were also with him other little ships. And there arose a great storm of wind and the waves beat into the ship, so that it was now full. And he was in the hinder part of the ship, asleep on a pillow: and they awake him and say unto him, Master, carest thou not that we perish? And he arose, and rebuked the wind, and said unto the sea, Peace, be still. And the wind ceased, and there was a great calm. And he said unto them, Why are ye so fearful? How is it that ye have no faith? And they feared exceedingly, and said one to another, What manner of man is this, that even the wind and the sea obey him."

St. Mark 4: 35-41

People spend little time thinking about this passage. It is an account of one of Jesus' miracles and it appears very simple. In fact, it is also symbolic: it is an account which gives us an image of the life of the disciple. The disciple is always on an ocean, in a boat where he has to face the tempest and the wind of his chaotic feelings and thoughts. The Christ is also in this boat, but he is sleeping. The disciple must awaken Him so that he can arise and say to the tumultuous feelings and thoughts, "Peace, Be still."

When he awoke, Jesus said to his disciples, "Why are ye so fearful? How is it that ye have no faith?" What does having faith mean? It means knowing that in the depths of our being lives a great power, a divine entity, the Christ. From the moment that Christ is found in our boat, we have nothing to fear; we shall not perish. Thanks to the presence of Christ, even if he is still sleeping, the boat will not be shipwrecked. We must really believe and know that there lives such a luminous and powerful Prince within us that all hostile forces are obliged to respect us; because of this divine presence in us we are in perfect safety.

When the Christ awakens within us, he will manifest his strength, his wisdom and his love, but even before he awakens we must *know* that he is on our boat and therefore be absolutely sure that we are risking nothing. That is what it is to have faith. Faith is believing something

The calming of the storm

which in appearance is unreal or even impossible. If you claim that you know something before believing it, you have knowledge, not faith. To have faith is to believe in something which you do not know, which you cannot see. Believing in God, believing in eternal life, that's faith.

We must always have faith, because in the spiritual, divine realm there are always things which one does not know, which one has not yet lived or seen. Faith is about the most subtle of things, those which are furthest from us and which cannot immediately be verified. You may argue that you know your wife, your children, your friends, and that you have faith in them. No, what you have there is confidence based on a certain experience; it is not faith. To have faith is to believe in something invisible, intangible. Even if we are not yet very evolved, even if the Christ has not awakened within us, it does not matter. What is necessary is faith, faith in order to surmount all the great tests of life.

Some readers are surprised that Jesus reproached his disciples; they feel that it was perfectly normal that those men should have been afraid of the storm and that, therefore, they should have awoken him. Yes, but for Jesus that fear was a lack of faith. They should have felt that since Jesus was with them, even if he was asleep, they were in no kind of danger. What merit would there have been in being unafraid if Jesus was with them, awake? They should have had faith even when he was asleep. Before Jesus awoke the disciples did not know that he would calm the storm. It was the first time that such an event had happened; the disciples had not yet seen Jesus speak to the elements. That is why after the miracle they spoke amongst themselves with astonishment, saying, "What manner of man is this, that even the wind and sea obey him?"

The Invisible World demands a faith from us similar to that which the disciples should have shown during the tempest. Since the Christ is in us, even if he is sleeping, we should remain peaceful, full of faith that though our boat may be storm tossed, it will not be shipwrecked. That is what it is to have faith: to believe without proof.

Within us all we have this precious treasure of the sleeping infant Christ. We should guard him carefully. He sleeps, he is very tiny, but one day, when he awakens, he will accomplish the most amazing feats. Let him go on sleeping but spread trust all around him. He is real, immortal. Meditate on what I have said to you and then you will discover that Jesus is sleeping in your little boat. If you awaken him, try not to

The calming of the storm

torment him with shabby little preoccupations and useless cries. "Why are ye so fearful? How is it that ye have no faith?" asks Jesus. Yes, one torments oneself for almost nothing at all and yet one never thinks that one has the greatest power within, the power of Christ.

Christ represents love, wisdom and truth within us. When great upheavals take place in our soul, everything will quickly become calm if we call for the help of love and wisdom. Wisdom is capable of making the clouds vanish and stilling the winds, whilst love makes the ocean calm. Wisdom acts on the wind (that is, on our thoughts) and love acts on the ocean of our feelings. Water and air, sea and wind, are eternal symbols. The apostles, who were aware of the meaning of symbols, only recorded in the Gospels those events where the details were significant on all planes. And it is because of this symbolic precision that generation after generation has been able to meditate on the events in the life of Jesus and his disciples.

8

THE FIRST SHALL BE LAST

"But many that are first shall be last; and the last shall be first.

"For the kingdom of heaven is like unto a man that is an householder, which went out early in the morning to hire labourers into his vineyard. And when he had agreed with the labourers for a penny a day, he sent them into his vineyard. And he went out about the third hour and saw others standing idle in the marketplace, and said unto them: Go ye also into the vineyard, and whatsoever is right I will give you. And they went their way. Again he went out about the sixth and ninth hour, and did likewise. And about the eleventh hour he went out, and found others standing idle, and said unto them, Why stand ye here all the day idle? They say unto him, Because no man hath hired us. He saith unto them, Go ye also into the vineyard; and whatsoever is right, that shall ye receive. So when even was come, the lord of the vineyard saith unto his steward, Call the labourers, and give them their hire, beginning from the last unto the first. And when they came that were hired about the eleventh hour, they received every man a penny. But when the first came, they supposed that they should have received more; and they likewise received every man a penny. And when they had received it, they murmured against the goodman of the house, saying, These last have wrought but one hour, and thou hast made them equal unto us, which have borne the burden and heat of the day. But he answered one of them and said, Friend, I do thee no wrong: didst not thou agree with me for a penny? Take that thine is and go thy way: I will give unto this last, even as unto thee. Is it not lawful for me to do what I will with mine own? Is thine eye evil, because I am good? So the last shall be first and the first last: for many be called but few chosen."

St. Matthew 19 : 30 and 20 : 1-16

In this account the attitude of the master of the house with regard to his workers may appear illogical, unjust and unreasonable. Most difficult to understand are the words, "Is it not lawful for me to do what I will with mine own?" Above all, if you consider the master of the house to represent God Himself, you would have to con-

The first shall be last

clude that God takes arbitrary decisions, doing what He likes without paying attention to anybody and clearly not acting according to the rules of justice! Why should those who had worked all day not be paid more than those who had only worked one hour? Why is it that the last became first and the first last? Are we therefore to understand that the most stupid of people will become the wisest, whereas the most wise will become fools? Does it mean that the rich will all become poor, whereas the beggars will all be transformed into multi-millionaires? If so, what joy for some and what a gloomy prospect for others! In fact, the truth is that Jesus, who talked in parables before the multitudes, revealed a great number of truths concerning human life and cosmic phenomena to his disciples. This parable must therefore be interpreted and not just taken at face value.

It says that the lord of the vineyard went out in the morning at the first hour, that he went again at the third, the sixth, the ninth and the eleventh hours. According to the Jews, the day was divided into twelve hours, beginning at six o'clock in the morning. The first hour then means six o'clock, the third eight o'clock, the sixth eleven o'clock, the ninth two o'clock and the eleventh four o'clock. Why were these particular hours chosen in the parable? The hours correspond to certain astrological data. First of all you must understand that at a given location the position of the sun is at a different height in the sky at six, eight, eleven and so on and also that at each of these hours a new constellation is in the ascendant. So then if one studied this parable from an astrological point of view, one would make very important discoveries, but that is not what I want to consider today.

One thing which you perhaps may not have thought of when reading this account is that the workers who were hired at different hours might not have had the same capacities or the same qualities. Nowadays, for example, we know that those who get up very early to go to work are the poor, whereas the rich can sleep until midday. That does not mean that in this parable you should take it that the workers in the first hour were poor and that those in the eleventh hour were rich, no, not at all, but by making this remark, I give you a method to use when you are studying such texts. Throughout the Gospels, Initiates are given little signs and pointers and so you must understand in this instance that the workers who came at different hours during the day did not all have the same abilities.

What counts in life for everyone is that they should come first, first in science, in the arts, in

The first shall be last

literature, in sport, first in beauty, skill, strength, riches, glory... the list is endless. Always and everywhere there is a first and there is a last also. However, if you wish to find out who is really the first and who is really the last, you will not be able to, because all human categories are relative. When you consider a limited number of individuals you can easily pick out the first and the last but, if you consider life as an infinite and uninterrupted chain, where are you going to find the first or the last? If you think of existence as a turning wheel, the one at the top of the wheel moves to the bottom and the one below moves up to the top. Imagine a family and then ask yourself who is the first, the father, the mother... or the child? Looked at from the point of view of age, the child is obviously the last, but in importance he is in first place because his father and mother think only of him, concentrating all their care on him. He may be the last to arrive on the scene yet, as he then becomes the centre of attention, in effect, he is the first! Or again, haven't you noticed that those who are the first when it is a question of wisdom, intelligence or knowledge, are often the last in strength and physical stamina, whereas others who are physically strong and sturdy have very little in their heads? That is the way things go in life. Those who are the first in one area are always the last in another area. Therefore rejoice, for each one of you can say that you are the first in some area or other.... It may, perhaps, be in bartering or in some rather dubious business but, nevertheless, you are the first!

Man possesses five senses, those of touch, taste, smell, hearing, and vision. The first to appear was the sense of touch and the last that of sight but, if we are looking at the organism – its structure and its capabilities – quite clearly sight is in first place in that it is the richest, the most subtle of all the senses. How do we explain this? Why does the sense that arrived first become the last in importance and the last the first? When you plant a seed, does it develop branches, flowers and fruit straightaway? Not at all, the roots develop first and then, when they are solidly established in the earth, the plant begins to grow, lifting its head above the soil until one day it produces flowers and fruit. The flowers and fruit arrive last. Even though the roots appeared first, they are quite clearly the last from the point of view of the organization of the plant in the scale of subtlety and beauty. Nobody bothers at all about roots; everyone is only interested in fruit and flowers. The poor old roots under the soil are forgotten and yet, from a biological point of view, they are the most important.

The first shall be last

In the field of love, it was sexuality, the instinct of procreation, which appeared first. Then after centuries a more spiritual form of love developed, as if the manifestations of sexual love had been nothing more than the roots of the plant which had developed enough to be able to produce branches, flowers and fruit. So primitive sexuality evolved into something increasingly complex and spiritualized. The more highly evolved a being is, the less can he be satisfied with animality; on the contrary, he increasingly seeks to manifest his love in beauty, wisdom and spirituality. The form of love which appeared first in the world now finds itself in last place because there has been an evolution. Therefore you see all these examples borrowed from different realms of existence go to show that nothing in Nature stays static but that everything is in movement, in evolution... and you will not understand the parable I just read if you do not grasp this idea of evolution.

In life, the man who always wants to stay in the same place without ever changing his level or his point of view will become the last, whereas the man who follows the currents of evolution can become the first. Suppose that you wanted to go all the way to the sun in a chariot drawn by oxen (always granting that a good path exists for your oxen from here!) how many thousands of years would you take on your journey? If you decided to travel by boat across the cosmic ocean you would take nearly as long. If you took the train you would get there quicker, even more quickly by plane. If you left with the speed of light, you would arrive in eight minutes and a few seconds. What do these examples mean? The man who goes by ox cart, who uses only the capabilities of his physical body, the old methods for resolving all his problems, will not find the solution for thousands of years. The one who voyages on water, going at the speed of ordinary feelings, will take just about as long to get to his goal. The one who travels by plane, using his intellect, will go quicker, but the one who can travel by spirit, by intuition, will move at the speed of light and will immediately find the truth.

If you want to be first in a motor race, don't use an old car! The cars which were the most perfect years ago have now been abandoned in the face of all the progress made on both bodywork and engines. You must pay attention to the evolution that has occurred in all areas of life in order to understand why Jesus said that the first shall be last. Prototypes cannot possess the highest degree of perfection. Many of our talents which now hold first place will, in the future, give way to new abilities and so become the last.

The first shall be last

One day a sixth sense will develop which will reveal an extraordinary universe to us, one which the first five senses were incapable of discovering.

Now let us look more closely at some of the details in this parable. We are told of a householder, lord of a vineyard, and of workers who were hired at different hours of the day, yet who all received the same salary regardless of the fact that the first had worked for twelve hours and the last for just one hour. This may appear unfair, yet we all accept that a stone breaker does not get the same salary as a painter of talent. A stone breaker may get 150 or 200 francs a day after working eight or ten hours whilst, with a few quick strokes of his brush, a painter who has taken half an hour to sketch your portrait can expect 1,000 or 10,000 francs. Such a difference is not uncommon; in many professions you can earn in half an hour much more than others do in a day's work. This difference in earnings proves that there are all sorts of different types of work and workers and we can come to the conclusion that the biblical workers, hired at different hours, did not all have the same capabilities.

Genesis begins with the words, "Bereschit bara Elohim eth ha-schamain ve-eth ha-arets" which translated means, "In the beginning God created the heaven and the earth". The word Elohim, which is translated as God, is in fact a plural formation. The Elohim are higher Beings who created Heaven and Earth with the help of many other entities, the "workers" of the parable. You must not think that before the creation of Heaven and Earth nothing existed. Before the appearance of our physical world and the creation of man, numerous Angelic Hierarchies existed who participated in the creation of our universe. The creation of Heaven and Earth which Genesis speaks of was only one moment in the infinity of Creation.

So then, the vineyard in this parable represents the world and the workers are all the different beings who came to participate in the great work of constructing it. If you re-read the Biblical account of the creation of the world you will see that on the first day God created light. "Vahii herev, vahii boqer, yom ehad": "And the evening and the morning were the first day". Have you asked yourself what was this day which began with the evening? It clearly must not be considered as one of our earthly days, but rather as a work period. On the second day, God created the firmament or foundation which would serve as the base for creation. On the third day, He commanded the earth to bring forth grass, the herb yielding seed... and the tree

The first shall be last

yielding fruit. The fourth day He created the sun, the moon and the stars. Given the fact that for us light comes from the sun and the stars, you may wonder how God was able to create them after the light. The answer, quite simply, is that the light which He created the first day was quite different from the visible light which comes to us from the heavenly bodies. The fifth day, God created the birds and the fishes; the sixth day He created animals and man and, finally, on the seventh day, He rested. This account in Genesis is a resumé of evolution.

When the master of the house (who, therefore, does not represent God Himself but the Elohim) wanted workers for his vineyard, he first of all called those who were capable of accomplishing the hardest, most difficult work. The first workers were therefore those beings who came down to work on the densest regions amongst the rocks, stones and earth. This period ran its course and then new workers were needed for different work, and so the master of the house called for the beings who entered the plants, trees and vegetables. When he came out for the third time the master called for those who worked with the bodies of animals, fish and birds, and they spread over the face of the earth, in the water and in the air. When the master went out for the fourth time, he hired much more evolved workers than the previous ones. These were intelligent beings, capable of working with matter and transforming it, and they took on human form. Finally, when the master went out for the last time, the work was practically finished in the vineyard, but he needed new workers to add the final perfect touches and so he called for beings who were even more highly evolved than all the others... the Angels. The arrival of Angels corresponds to the development of consciousness in man. They came last in order to complete creation.

Yes, you see, you do not give Angels work to do in the mineral world. This cruder level of work is done by others. You can see the same thing around you all the time. Kings or Heads of State do not come to sweep the town's streets. In a factory, the one who arrives latest, the manager, often has no function other than giving his signature yet, with these signatures, he earns more than the workers because he is making essential decisions for the running of the factory. He signs, and then he is free... but what a lot of work he first had to do in order to be able, one day, to reach this position of having no more to do than append his signature.

You must understand that the level of evolution, capacities and virtues are not the same in all people. Let us look at what happens in our

The first shall be last

bodies, made up as they are of different systems. The first is the bone structure, the skeleton, a solid framework which hardly changes during its lifetime. That skeleton can be compared to the mineral kingdom: it represents the workers of the first hour. The second group of workers is represented by the muscular system; this system evolves very little in the course of its existence and it corresponds to the kingdom of vegetables whose roots are deeply buried in the earth of the skeletal system. The third group of workers is represented by the circulatory and respiratory systems: they correspond to the animal kingdom which moves on earth, in water and in the air. The fourth group of workers corresponds to the nervous system which was developed much later in man. As this is a more subtle structure than the preceding ones, it can have many variations. The fifth group of workers corresponds to the entities which work on the spiritual side of our being, on our aura which is also an organism, a system, but an extraordinarily subtle system. These workers represent the Angelic Kingdom.

So then how do the first become the last? Quite simply, by not evolving. All beings who stay content with making use of their most elementary capabilities (those which correspond to the skeletal, muscular, circulatory and respiratory systems) do not evolve. Whereas those who use the capabilities of the spirit evolve rapidly and become the first because, by using these capabilities, they outstrip others. Many other beings will come to develop other qualities and thanks to these qualities, they will take first place.

So now you can see how the first will be the last and the last will be the first. At first glance, this parable was completely unreasonable, but once you think about it, it all becomes perfectly clear and logical. The workers of the first hour were not the most gifted. That is why, even though they worked the longest, they did not receive a higher salary than those workers of the eleventh hour, who accomplished a much more subtle and delicate task.

There was therefore no injustice. All were paid in a perfectly just and wise way, yet in the parable it says that when they received their pay, the workers who were hired in the first hour, "...murmured against the goodman of the house". Their complaint showed that they had not understood the laws of evolution. If they had not wanted to be superceded they had only to work! There are two ways to work if you do not want others to be ahead of you, you can work with love and you can work with wisdom. These methods help you to advance very quickly.

The first shall be last

When you see someone who is wiser than you, instead of being unhappy, jealous and wanting to slander, draw near, watch the way he works, find out how he achieves such good results. You will learn a great deal this way. Suppose you have made a lot of effort without getting results, say to yourself, "I will go near this man who has reached such a high level of evolution and then I will discover the secret of his success." In this way, by going to look for a real Master, you will learn much.

If you are a musician, go to hear those whose extraordinary concerts attract the crowds. Leave your pride behind, for your pride will teach you nothing! Go and watch how this genius plays, ask him who his teacher was, ask how he works, but never, never, argue defiantly because it is in that sort of rebellion that you will become the last. Neither rebellion nor anger can help you, but only love and wisdom. If you fear that another might be ahead of you, or if you are jealous that they are, you have neither love nor wisdom. Those who love are never uneasy or jealous, for they feel rich. A rich man has no need to be jealous. Only the poor are jealous because they feel that they have nothing.

If you want to become the first, study, meditate, work with love and wisdom, and then you will surpass all others. You will overtake them so quickly that they will not even have the time to hear you say "Hello!" because you will have already shot so far ahead. It is by working with love and wisdom that one travels through space at the speed of light.

9

THE PARABLE OF THE FIVE WISE AND THE FIVE FOOLISH VIRGINS

"Then shall the kingdom of heaven be likened unto ten virgins, which took their lamps, and went forth to meet the bridegroom. And five of them were wise, and five were foolish. They that were foolish took their lamps, and took no oil with them. But the wise took oil in their vessels with their lamps. While the bridegroom tarried, they all slumbered and slept. And at midnight, there was a cry made, Behold the bridegroom cometh: go ye out to meet him. Then all those virgins arose, and trimmed their lamps. And the foolish said unto the wise, Give us of your oil; for our lamps are gone out. But the wise answered saying, Not so; lest there be not enough for us and you: but go ye rather to them that sell, and buy for yourselves. And while they went to buy, the bridegroom came; and they that were ready, went in with him to the marriage: and the door was shut. Afterward came also the other virgins, saying, Lord, Lord, open to us. But he answered and said, Verily I say unto you, I know you not. Watch therefore, for ye know neither the day nor the hour wherein the Son of man cometh."

St. Matthew 25 : 1-13

In reading this parable you cannot help noticing how odd some of the details are. For example, each guest has been told to bring a lighted lamp to the marriage. It would appear then that the hall is in darkness and so each one must bring his own light! Have you ever seen such a thing? Another incomprehensible detail is the cruelty of the bridegroom who did not hesitate to shut the door right in the faces of the five virgins who had no oil, despite the fact that they had come specially to meet him. Was their crime so great that they deserved such punishment? What a disagreeable and ill-bred fellow this bridegroom must be, waking everyone up in the dead of night and then leaving five poor girls outside on the pretext that they haven't got any oil in their lamps! Is it really worth the bother of waiting for such an obnoxious man who makes such dramas over a little bit of oil?

Such bizarre details are found everywhere in the parables, but it is in these very details that Initiates discover proof of the deep wisdom of the Gospels. Faced with all the contradictions

The parable of the five wise virgins... 137

and absurdities of this parable one is forced to conclude that lamp, oil, bridegroom and even the virgins are all symbols which need interpretation.

Let us start with the virgins: there are five wise and five foolish virgins. Why in this parable has Jesus chosen the number five? Why not four or six? It is because the number five is that of the five fundamental virtues: goodness, justice, love, wisdom and truth. The five wise virgins represent these virtues whereas the five foolish virgins represent the corresponding defects.

Since Jesus has presented these virtues and these vices as people, we can make their acquaintance. Let us begin with the foolish virgins.

Our first virgin is deficient in goodness. Preoccupied completely and solely with satisfying her own desires and ambitions, she follows her path without noticing the people she meets along the way, either ignoring or crushing them. If she says anything at all, it is only to say wicked things; her malevolence and spite make her detested by all.

The second virgin is one who commits all sorts of injustice, provoking agitation wherever she goes, yet claiming all the time that others are responsible. Whenever she suffers for any particular reason she is always convinced of her perfect guiltlessness and so accuses everyone else, family, friends, society, and even God Himself. Surely if He were just He would never send anything but happiness and success her way!

The third virgin has nothing but hatred for others and that is why she is always unhappy. All she does is to shout and get angry as if her only desire were to make life totally unbearable for those near her. The one thing which makes her happy is to hear of the disasters that befall other people.

The fourth virgin is completely unreasonable; she rushes into everything at top speed, never taking time to think about the results of her actions. You cannot confide any secrets in her because she repeats them to all and sundry, even to those whom you had especially asked her not to inform. Her behaviour produces catastrophes in the life of others, not because she is wicked, only because she is so totally thoughtless she is incapable of one good action. When she is happy, there's something very disagreeable about her way of showing it, and even when she cries she makes such a performance out of it, moaning and groaning so loudly she attracts everyone's attention. Totally lacking in discernment, she takes stupid people for intelligent and vice versa and, besides, she is quite incapable of hearing what other people have to say!

The fifth virgin excels in the art of lying.

Telling stories is her greatest pleasure. She gets enormous delight from being a boundless source of rumour and invention which others swallow. Inevitably the time comes when she believes all her inventions; a victim of her own imagination, living in a world of illusion and lies.

I have not given you the names of the five foolish virgins because, if they stay in your memory, they might have a bad effect on you. However I will tell you the names of the five wise virgins.

The first virgin was called Tova. She was very good, she ran everywhere to help others and that is the reason she had very pretty feet. Right from her earliest childhood, Tova learnt to be good. She was an orphan living with her grand-parents who loved her very much. Her grandmother spent a great deal of time with her, showing her the flowers, the fruit, the insects and teaching her how to love and look after them. She was always thinking of giving a helping hand. She looked after the children of the neighbourhood, consoled the unhappy and distributed wealth to the poor. That is why everyone loved her.

The second virgin was called Tsadka. Tsadka had a very great sense of justice which she had inherited from her father who, though severe, was very just. Even though he preferred Tsadka, he never showed it so as not to make her arrogant. He distributed everything equally, thus giving his favourite daughter her first lesson in justice. She observed her father and tried to imitate him. She also watched and noted all the different ways life manifests itself. Because of her great discernment she understood that people's sufferings are not random but exist because they are the results of their previous faults. She was full of wonder towards the laws which govern the world.

The third virgin was called Ahava. Her father was forced to leave the family to look for work abroad and so all the family were left in their mother's care. Ahava, who saw all the sacrifices her mother made for her family, was overwhelmed by such evidence of love. She greatly admired her mother and she, too, wanted to sacrifice herself for others. Often when she went out for walks she looked up at the sun, the clouds, the birds, and sent them all her love. She smiled at children and even when they were naughty with her, she still supported them and looked after them tenderly. So of course the children loved her more and more, always wanting her to smile at them and notice them and treat them tenderly for, when she spoke, her voice and her words were a caress.

The parable of the five wise virgins...

The fourth virgin was called Hokmah. She was nearly always silent, quite happy to watch, reflect and listen, always silently. Sometimes, as a child, it was impossible to find her because she had gone to visit an Initiate who lived not very far from her. She asked him many questions because she wanted to learn and had never yet found anybody able to give replies to all the questions which preoccupied her. She understood how profound life is, how complex, and saw that it is directed by omnipresent reason. She saw that everything in Nature is linked and began to discover the corresponding phenomena in herself and related her thoughts, feelings and actions with the seasons, the rain, the stars and the flowers....

At first, Hokmah's parents were not very pleased with her. They scolded her for filling the house with stones, shells, insects and all sorts of "rubbish" but Hokmah either said nothing or said, "Let me carry on, I'm so happy studying and making such fascinating discoveries". Later on, her parents learnt that she was visiting the Initiate and Hokmah began to teach them many things and she did the same to her friends and all those around her.

Hokmah had a remarkable quality: she knew how to listen. She listened to the Initiate with extraordinary attention and respect. She also listened to all the sounds of nature, the running of the streams, the falling rain, the wind in the trees. Very often she would lie on the ground to hear the noises of the forest and so discovered more and more about that Voice which lives and speaks in everything.

The fifth virgin was called Amena. She was born at a very favourable hour when Sun, Moon and Mercury were all very well aspected. When Amena looked at you, you felt so strongly how clear, open and frank everything was in her. She hid nothing, as she had nothing to hide. She was born like this, bearing witness to the truth, because in her previous incarnations she had been truthful and so now she was linked to the world of truth. This link enabled her to choose her family for this incarnation, as she was already free. The bringer of truth is not subject to the law of Karma but can freely choose both family and conditions in which to be born. He takes on only the good qualities of his parents but he brings this higher virtue with him. When Amena looked at people they immediately felt that the world of truth really does exist; her eyes emanated such light that under its influence they felt comforted and calmed. Amena also loved contemplation. She looked up at Heaven, at the mountains and the sea, she loved looking at the stars at night, too, and often got up to admire

The parable of the five wise virgins...

them. Then she linked herself at that moment to the entire universe and her soul travelled worlds without end, through limitless space. When she looked up at the stars she could read the heavenly writing in them because she understood that they represent characters inscribed by the Lord in His living book of Nature. In springtime she got up very early to see the sunrise. Her greatest quality was her need for contemplation, for adoration. Jesus took the sister of Lazarus as model for the fifth virgin because Mary used to look at him all the time, linking herself to the spirit of truth.

So, there your are. I have introduced you to the five foolish virgins and the five wise virgins. You will no doubt find that this is all a little fanciful and you are right; however, symbolically it is exact.

Let us move on now to the lamps that these virgins had to bring in order to light the banqueting hall. Nowadays we no longer need oil lamps but, used as symbols, oil and lamps have an important role in our lives. Suppose, for example, that you are anaemic, your vital force has diminished, you are somnolent and exhausted. What has happened is that the lamp of your body lacks oil and is beginning to go out. The lamp is then taken to hospital; to help the flickering flame, a little bit of oil is added and the flame begins to shine more brightly. The oil in this example is blood. Imagine now that you need food and clothing. Without oil in your lamp (or in this case, money in your pocket) you cannot buy anything. Go into your garden and see a flower which is drying out... give it a little water and once again it blossoms. So throughout life, everywhere, in all areas we can find "oil" and "lamps": the stomach's "oil" is food, for the lungs it is air, for the brain it is ideas.

Therefore oil is found everywhere. Plants find it in the soil, in the air and in the rays of the sun and with it they prepare their sap, symbol of that living sap which also flows within us, in the solar plexus. The solar plexus is the reservoir of our vital forces, it is the accumulator of all energies. If you know how to replenish it every day, you will have a source which you can draw upon for the forces which you need at every moment. Your lamp will provide you with all you need whilst you wait for Him, the bridegroom the virgins awaited, to come to you each day in the form of light, wisdom, inspiration and love.

Oil symbolizes the vital force, the sap which nourishes all the cells. You have already lived through many experiences and you will have noticed that if you have behaved with wisdom, goodness, generosity and self-control for one

The parable of the five wise virgins...

week, you will have acquired the ability to face the problems which come in the following days much more easily. You deal with them as if you have a support, a help within you, some kind of energy which has been prepared in the cells of your nervous system which protects you by its strength so that you can stand up to the greatest tension. Something has been developed in you which gives you that ability to resist shocks and difficulties. The man who lives a sensible life, one which is luminous and full of love, feels a force welling up in him, a force which is like the oil of the lamp and, even when he is tired and ill, if he knows how to rest quietly for a moment, he will feel this force working within him which will restore him. If this force did not exist within his cells, he would not be able to withstand and survive.

You can now see that this parable of the ten virgins has a much wider and deeper sense than it has been previously given. For the Initiates the meaning is perfectly clear and when in the parable Jesus talked of the wise and the foolish virgins it was because the solar plexus is in relation with the astrological sign of Virgo. When Jesus said, "Out of his belly shall flow rivers of living water", he was referring to the solar plexus. So if we live, think and feel correctly, our solar plexus is able to distribute living forces to our cells, making and keeping us healthy, vigorous and full of energy.

The five wise and five foolish virgins represent two categories of human beings, both men and women, those who know how to prepare the oil in their lamps and those who do not. Sometimes you spend all your energy in anger, in argument or amusement and then when the bridegroom comes (in the form of magnificent experiences or Higher Beings), you are not prepared to understand, follow, or love Him: you are feeble, ill, exhausted and you suffer because you do not have the strength to meet these Beings or to live these experiences to the full and so you find yourself deprived of all blessings.

To a certain degree this kind of thing can happen every day. For example, imagine that yesterday you were in a very bad inner state: today your face is not luminous and open and you do not feel at your best. Then you are invited to a party where you are to meet remarkable and important people and you are very sad that you cannot be introduced to them looking your most radiant. Oh yes, there are receptions to which one can be invited totally unexpectedly: if you are in a bad frame of mind and you nonetheless decide to go, no one will find you pleasant company. Despite your finery and your jewels, peo-

The parable of the five wise virgins...

ple will flee from you, instinctively reacting to your sombreness, your lack of light, and so to a certain extent you will be excluded from the occasion. Physically you will be there but you will not be able to participate with your whole consciousness as you had not prepared the oil to fill your solar plexus, that oil which is distilled only by slow constant effort over a long period.

Let me give you another example. Imagine that you find yourself outside a theatre or concert hall and you want to go in and see the performance. You go to the ticket office and you say to the man there, "I have the most distinguished parents, you have certainly heard of them, so kindly let me into the auditorium." The employee will reply, "We have never heard of them, you must pay for your entrance ticket like anyone else." You can shout and complain as much as you like, it will make no difference, you will not be accepted and will have to stay outside. Wherever you go, whether to a ball or a banquet, you will not be allowed in if you are not able to pay for your entrance ticket. Obviously this is all symbolic: the ball, the concert, the banquet to which one is refused entry if one cannot pay, symbolize – quite simply – true life. From now on this true life is open to you, too, and you may join the Initiates, Angels and Archangels assembled there. But to be admitted to their company, you must be like the five wise virgins: you must manifest justice, wisdom, goodness, love and truth.

All those who possess these five virtues can enter this new life because they have entrance tickets. Whereas without these virtues, however rich, wise or celebrated you are, you will not be able to enter. You will be told, "Yes, you are known at the Academy, the Sorbonne, Parliament... but if you do not have your ticket bearing the words goodness, justice, wisdom, love and truth, you are not recognized here." The first word is represented by the feet (goodness), the second by the hands (justice), the third by the mouth (love), the fourth by the ears (wisdom) and the fifth by the eyes (truth) and, according to what is written on your ticket, the bridegroom will either chase you away or will welcome you into the wedding feast amidst singing and dancing.

In this celebration each person must find his place and sing. It is not a question of singing whatever you please... not at all! All those who take part are predestined to sing a predetermined tune: the choirs sing in five parts and these five voices are written on the five lines of the stave. On the first line is goodness; on the second, justice; on the third, love; on the fourth, wisdom; and on the fifth, truth. Each be-

The parable of the five wise virgins...

ing is predestined to hold one of these five melodic lines which he will have to learn in the course of his earthly life. Each virtue has its own particular tune.

As for the five foolish virgins who never wanted to learn any of the tunes of these five virtues, they will be sent away. Of course when that happens they will go to the five wise virgins to ask for a little of their oil. However, true oil cannot be given and you will not find it for sale on the open market. You can only obtain it by the constant sacrifice and gift of yourself. Nature gives us a little of this oil in our food and in the air but, above all, it is we who must learn how to prepare it in ourselves by our thoughts and feelings.

The five foolish virgins who did not have time to prepare the oil for their lamps were not allowed to go in with the bridegroom. When he said, "Verily I say unto you, I know you not", he meant, "You have not prepared your oil, you come here today for the first time; you have made no efforts, had no spiritual experiences in your life; I do not know you, I have never seen you, so off you go!" The bridegroom is not cruel, but he does refuse to be disturbed by foolish men and women! You all know how harsh Nature is: when we have spent the most precious energies which she has given us, she leaves us weak, without strength, and is in no hurry to give us our energy back again. If we fall ill, the convalescence is often very long and often it is quite impossible to re-establish perfect health. Can one blame Nature for her cruelty when it is we who do not behave in a reasonable manner?

It is interesting to compare this parable of the wise and foolish virgins with an episode in the Gospels which also has never been properly interpreted: the story of the cursing of the barren fig tree.... "And on the morrow, when they were come from Bethany, he was hungry; And seeing a fig tree afar off having leaves, he came, if haply he might find any thing thereon: and when he came to it, he found nothing but leaves; for the time of figs was not yet. And Jesus answered and said unto it, No man eat fruit of thee hereafter for ever. And his disciples heard it.... And in the morning as they passed by, they saw the fig tree dried up from the roots." (St. Mark 11 : 12-14, 20)

If you take this anecdote literally, you could well ask if Jesus had behaved in a good and rational way. What right had he to demand that a tree should bear fruit when it wasn't even the right season for fruit? It has to be understood that, just as we saw in the parable of the wise and foolish virgins that the oil of their lamps did not represent material oil so, in the same way,

The parable of the five wise virgins...

neither does the fig tree here represent a tree. The tree represents a human being and in people the same periods and seasons do not exist. At any given moment we must be capable of bearing fruit (in other words luminous thoughts and warm feelings), for the Lord may come at any moment. He does not wait for a particular period; nor does He announce His coming in advance. When He comes, whether it is winter or summer, day or night, man's tree must be able to bear fruit, otherwise the spirit will abandon him and to be abandoned by the spirit is to be cursed so that the tree that is man will wither, losing his energies, his vitality, becoming decrepit. Just as we must always have oil in our lamps, we must also always be able to produce fruit in our minds and hearts, souls and spirits.

The same idea is found in the parable of the talents, that story of the master who, before he left on his travels, distributed his talents amongst his servants. On his return he rewarded those who had made their talents blossom and he punished those who were content with merely burying theirs.

"Watch therefore, for ye know neither the day nor the hour", says the bridegroom. This is a very important phrase. "Watch", does not mean, "Do not go to sleep", for all the virgins were asleep, the wise as well as the foolish, and the parable does not say that that was a fault. "Watch", means always to be awake spiritually, for you do not know the day or the hour the bridegroom will come. The bridegroom comes each day, and the days when our lamps are not filled with oil are days when we cannot enter to share in the banquet to which he has invited us. When you do have this oil, you enter the banqueting hall and you are transported with joy: everybody around you is amazed and wonders what has happened to make you so gloriously, shiningly happy. Unfortunately, the bridegroom does not stay a long time because people have not learnt how to keep Him; they do not know how to preserve this state of wonder in themselves over a long period.

Even though we now use electricity, we find that the symbol of oil lamps is as valid today as it was in the past. If we see the light (or bulb) as representing our intellect, our spirit, then the electricity can represent the oil, that essential liquid without which the light would go out. Where does this living oil come from? It is provided by a central generating board. If the lamp (our intellect) is not plugged into this central grid (the Lord, our Heavenly Father), our spirit will go out. The secret which allows us to obtain this miraculous oil is that we must make that connection to the Lord by prayer, meditation and

The parable of the five wise virgins... 153

contemplation. If we keep the current switched on the oil will flow into us, our lamps will be lighted and their flames will shine steadily brighter and brighter. Initiates represent spiritual lamps whereas ordinary people who are not connected to the Invisible World live in darkness and the problems of their lives remain insoluble.

Jesus spoke of foolish or wise virgins but this obviously does not mean that you should think it is only women who are concerned! The same thing goes for men, who are just as capable of showing folly or wisdom. Yes, on the spiritual plane men are also either wise virgins or foolish virgins. Certain saints, certain mystics have worked over the years trying to fill their lamps for the day when the Beloved, the Bridegroom comes in order that they might charm Him. This beloved, this mystic Bridegroom, is the Holy Spirit. Anybody, whether male or female, who is capable of accumulating this spiritual oil within by prayer, meditation and a pure chaste life, will one day be visited by the Holy Spirit. Jesus used the word "virgin" because he was talking of the human soul: the soul, whether in a man or a woman, is always a young girl, a virgin who has to have a receptive attitude if she is to attract this subtle element which pervades the world and is spread throughout the atmosphere. This element is found only in infinitesimal doses and so each day you must lay in your provisions, drop by drop, so that no matter what happens you will always have some in reserve. The foolish virgin is not called foolish because she does foolish things, but because of her folly in not foreseeing that one must prepare reserves for the future.

You all know the story of Joseph and Pharaoh. In his dream Pharaoh saw seven fat cows and then seven lean cows who ate the fat cows. As he did not understand the meaning of this dream he asked Joseph to explain it. Joseph interpreted it thus: "There will be seven fat or prosperous years for the kingdom of Egypt, but they will be followed by seven years of sterility and famine. Therefore, my advice is that you should prepare huge barns in which you can store the greater part of the harvest gathered during the seven years of abundance. When the period of scarcity comes, Egypt will be the granary of the world; it will sell its reserves to other countries and so become very rich." Pharaoh followed his advice and everything happened exactly as Joseph had predicted.

If such events can happen for a group or nation the same thing can occur on a personal level: fluctuations are always happening in your life. Some days are fertile and abundant and then there are a few days which are barren, fol-

The parable of the five wise virgins...

lowed once again by fertile days. If you are like the foolish virgins you take no precautions and then complain loudly, "It's all so barren and dry! I have nothing anymore, no joy, no inspiration, nothing!" If, instead of wasting your riches you had known how to foresee the difficult period (just as the waning moon follows the waxing moon) you would have stored up a few provisions, a little magnetism, a little of this oil and then those days of the waning moon would have been just as beneficial and fertile as the other days.

You can verify (as I have done) the profundity and the truth of all these analogies and all these symbolic interpretations for yourselves. People do not know how to be thrifty, intelligent, using foresight to store wealth for the days which are to come. There is a French proverb which says, "Keep a pear for when you are thirsty." You can find in proverbs traces of the age-old wisdom which was spread by the Initiates of the past. They were very intelligent beings with a very deep knowledge of cycles and periods; they knew of the alternating phases of prosperity and penury, of abundance and want, and so they gave this advice.

As for the bridegroom of whom Jesus speaks in this parable, this Bridegroom for whom one should prepare, he is the Holy Spirit. It is for

Him that you should have oil, because He is a flame and a flame needs to be fed. The flame is the bridegroom and the oil is its nourishment. Without oil, the light goes out. The bridegroom is the light and the Holy Spirit is none other than the Bridegroom of Light. However, Light does not come unless you have enough oil to nourish its flame. Now you can understand why, fifty days after Easter, the disciples received the Holy Spirit in the form of flames, in tongues of fire which burned over their heads: it was because they had oil.

Now I will present this parable to you in its practical light. If, with the five virgins (the fingers of your right hand) you touch the lamp (your solar plexus) and you meditate on noble and divine ideas, you will fill this lamp with forces and energies which you can use later. When you feel happy, filled with energy, do not waste it all in useless gestures, words, thoughts and feeling, but do what I have just told you: put your right hand on your solar plexus whilst meditating and silently fill it with this strength, this joy.

Here is another method. Choose a big tree –an oak, beech, or birch – and put your back against it, holding your left hand with its palm against the tree trunk behind your back and the palm of your right hand on your solar plexus.

Concentrate on the energy of the tree which you try to receive with your left hand and then send that energy through your organism with your right hand. After several minutes of this exercise you will feel yourself strengthened, calmed and even healed. However, in order to receive this transfusion of energy properly you must first be taught. If you really know how to appreciate it, you will find this method has extraordinary value.

Instead of trying to prepare the alchemist's oil, in search of which people have vainly given their health and fortune, it is much better to go into a forest and talk to the trees. However, if you are to talk to them, you must first be aware that they are living beings and you must love them. Thanks to the understanding and love of the trees, you will establish a subtle harmony and communion with Nature. Very few people nowadays have any idea of the prodigious energy which the trees of the forest possess. Communication with the spirits of the trees was an art possessed by the Druids but now man has lost the secret of how to regenerate himself and no longer understands the universal language. Once again he must discover the living book of Nature. Take yourself into forests, walk through Nature, give yourself new life, and praise the Lord who created such wonders and splendours.

You can also build up your stocks of this oil by nutrition, by meditation and prayer. By eating with great care and much love you will be able to extract the quintessence of food in the same way that the essential oil of roses is extracted: just a very few grammes are extracted from an enormous quantity of petals. By breathing you also absorb other very subtle elements, and by meditation and prayer you extract even more subtle elements. When you possess this quintessence a perfume emanates from you and you then attract all the spiritual entities, beings who come, marvelling, towards you.... Finally it is the Bridegroom Himself who is attracted and comes to visit you, the most wonderful Bridegroom of all, the Holy Spirit. Once the Holy Spirit has installed Himself within you, not only will His light help you see everything, but you will also have His warmth; for His light is also a flame.

10

"THIS IS LIFE ETERNAL, THAT THEY MIGHT KNOW THEE THE ONLY TRUE GOD"

I

"These words spake Jesus and lifted up his eyes to heaven and said, Father, the hour is come; glorify thy Son, that thy Son also may glorify thee: As thou hast given him power over all flesh, that he should give eternal life to as many as thou hast given him. And this is life eternal, that they might know thee the only true God and Jesus Christ, whom thou hast sent."

St. John 17: 1-3

All those who have meditated on these verses of St. John's Gospel, and in particular on the last, have wondered what is meant by this strange link between a knowledge of God and eternal life. How can knowing God give eternal life? What links are there between our day-to-day existence and life without end? Some have thought that the phrase "to know God" is only a manner of speech which hides no difficult concept. They think that, in order to know God, one need only read theological treatises, philosophical, gnostic, kabbalistic or alchemical texts which explain God's attributes, describe His power, outline how He created the world... that it is enough merely to know that God is love, wisdom, truth, justice and so on in order to know Him. However this approach does not explain the link between knowing God and His Son and possessing eternal life. The whole question of knowledge itself is not at all clear. Philosophy and psychology deal with it, so does biology which studies the structure of neurones, their different functions and the connections which exist between the different centres of the brain and the nervous system. But in spite of all these discoveries, the capacity for knowledge, the act of knowing, still remain a mystery.

Life is nothing but a series of learning processes. People try to have relationships with rich, wise and influential men or with beautiful women but what results will come from getting to know these people? People read all sorts of books to be up to date but the things they learn are often poisonous and their whole life can be turned into hell.... What is behind this need to know and understand? Very often there is a selfish motive: people think that they can gain something whereas, in fact, quite the opposite

"This is life eternal..."

occurs. The fly looks curiously at the spider's web, it wants to know all about it, it is quite sure that at the centre of this network of filaments lives a very intelligent being who has constructed this web. If the fly ventures in, it will indeed get to know the spider but it will lose everything in the process. The artist who built the trap will be delighted, but it will be the end of the fly! Spiders' webs and traps are spread everywhere for us and so it is not advisable to touch, feel and taste everything on the pretext that you want to know what it is.

I have often told you that in order to know it is not enough merely to read, study, analyse and reflect. True knowledge, true understanding, is not only theoretic and intellectual, but also consists in touching and tasting the object you want to know, so that you unite and blend into it. All knowledge that is only intellectual stays external and superficial: one does not know people or things unless one fuses into them. What does the word "know" mean in the Bible? For example it says, "And Adam knew Eve... Abraham knew Sarah...." Yes, and each time a child was born. Therefore true knowledge consists of coming into contact and fusing with what one wants to know.

Look at a little child: he wants to know his world and so he touches everything, putting everything he comes across into his mouth. You also get to know things by using your ears, nose and eyes. In order really to know anything it is necessary that at least a few elements within us vibrate in harmony with what we want to know. If we are not prepared, if our hearts and minds are not in a certain state of inner attentiveness, receptive and ready to respond to vibrations both within and without, there is no chance of our gaining knowledge. We may pretend that we want to know very evolved invisible beings, but it is quite impossible unless we have learnt to respond to the vibrations they produce. Once our souls know how to vibrate in harmony with these beings, we will immediately know them.

If we are to achieve knowledge, two elements are absolutely essential: one is active and positive and one passive and negative; in other words, one masculine and the other feminine. These two elements have to unite in order to interpenetrate each other for this is the way life is constructed. If we want to understand something it is necessary to be penetrated by it. If we want to know it by tasting it, we must take it and put it in our mouth; if we want to smell it, we must absorb some of its particles through our noses. If we want to know it by our ears, sound waves

"This is life eternal..."

have to enter the auditory canals and so on.... If we want to know the cosmic Spirit, we have to let it penetrate us.

"This is life eternal, that they might know thee, the only true God and Jesus Christ, whom thou hast sent." In the kabbalistic tradition, the essence of God is contained in the four letters of His name, יהוה Yod Hé Vau Hé. These four letters correspond to the four principles which work in man; the spirit, the soul, the intellect and the heart. Yod י is the creative masculine principle, that holy primordial force which is at the origin of all movement, the spirit. The second letter Hé ה, represents the feminine principle, the soul which absorbs, conserves, protects and permits the creative principle to work in her. The third letter, Vau ו, represents the son who is born from the union of the first two principles, the masculine and feminine, the father and the mother. It is the first child of the union and it is also manifested as an active principle, though on another level. The son is the intellect which follows in the footsteps of his father, Yod, the spirit, and you can see that the shape of the letter Vau ו is the same as that of Yod י, only lengthened. The following letter, the Hé ה, is identical to the second letter which, as I have already said, is the soul, the mother. It represents the heart, the daughter, who is a repetition of the mother.* Therefore the four letters of the Name of God represent the spirit (the father), the soul (the mother), the intellect (the son) and the heart (the daughter). If the spirit dominates in you, you resemble the father; if it is the soul, then your qualities are those of the mother. If the intellect has first place you are like the son and if it is the heart, you are like the daughter.

These four principles are found in the face, for man's face is made in the image of God. The eyes represent Yod, the spirit; the ears Hé, the soul; the nose represents the Vau, the intellect and the mouth represents the second Hé, the heart.

So then, to sum up, there are four forces which are all related:

* The Kabbala looks upon the Name of God as a chart or diagram of the family cell. This interpretation of the Vau and the second Hé, or the similarity between father and son, mother and daughter, is corroborated in practically the same terms by Dr. C. G. Jung in his psychological papers on the degree and scope of parenthood. In *Modern Man in Search of Soul*, Dr. Jung discusses his conclusions concerning the degrees of similarity between members of the same family based on the results of Tests by Association: between father and son the difference is 3, 1... the close connection between father and son is an established fact, the son having always been considered the incarnation of his father. And between a mother and daughter the difference is 3, the least recorded difference, the daughter being the repetition, the replica of her mother. (editor's note)

"This is life eternal..." 167

    י Yod, the spirit, corresponds to the eyes,
    ה Hé, the soul, corresponds to the ears,
    ו Vau, the intellect, corresponds to the nose,
    ה Hé, the heart, corresponds to the mouth.

These four energies, therefore, represent the four senses of sight, hearing, smell and taste. The fifth sense is that of touch, the hands with which we work. To the four letters of the Name of God, add a fifth letter, the shin ש, which one finds at the heart of the name of Jesus, Jeschuah יהשוה. This name is the symbol of formation, of the incarnation of God in matter. Through Jesus, the Christ, the spirit, soul, intellect and heart of God incarnate on the physical plane so that God can become visible, tangible: he is the Word made flesh. Christ is the Incarnation of God in matter, it is Christ who gives the four divine principles their manifestation. It is also represented by the hand for the five fingers represent those five virtues of love, wisdom, truth, justice and goodness which are placed on the branches of the pentagram, symbol of perfect man.

Jesus is the son of God descended here on earth to show us how we should act. If we remain with the spirit, the soul, the intellect and the heart, without manifesting them on the physical plane, we do not know the Lord. Perhaps we will know Him when we leave for the

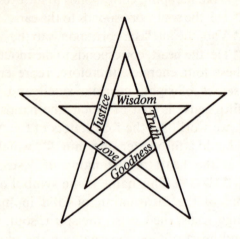

other side, but that will do us no good at all... it will be too late. It is here on earth that we should know Him so that we can taste eternal life. We have a spirit, a soul, an intellect and a heart but that is not enough, we must also manifest their qualities through the physical body. Jesus is manifested through the work of our hands. He said, "My Father works and I work with Him." In other words, my Father works everywhere, through brains, hearts, souls and spirits and I, too, work amongst people here, in matter, with my hands.

People have made the whole question of eternal life so incredibly abstract that they don't realize that all the necessary elements are there, in their eyes, ears, noses, mouths and hands, to enable them to live in this state now. The more you are considerate towards your five senses, the more you pay attention to the way you use them, the nearer you will draw to the knowledge of those supreme truths which no book, no philosopher, can ever reveal to you. The revelation will come from within you yourself, it is absolutely clear and true, it will never deceive you and it is the result of the correct usage of your five senses.

"This is life, eternal, that they might know thee, the only true God...." To achieve eternal life is to succeed in creating a link by opening our spirits, souls, intellects, hearts and wills to all the virtues of the Name of God* and to His Son, the Christ. We will then be fed from an inexhaustible supply, by a central source of energy, just as a light bulb is fed by the current from a generator. Let us therefore open our hearts through the means of purity.... Let us open our intellects through light.... Let us open our souls through spiritual love.... Let us open our spirit through the strength and the power of God and let us accomplish the Will of our Lord, the Christ!

---

* For more on the Name of God, see Chapter I of *The True Meaning of Christ's Teaching,* Izvor 215.

We will not get to know God and the Christ with our intellect and its artificial constructions: we can only do so by purifying all our faculties. If you want to know how you should purify them, I would tell you to look at the way water purifies itself in Nature. There are two possible processes... in the first one, the water penetrates the soil and goes through different layers, leaving its impurities behind. In this way, little by little, it becomes clear and then it will bubble up elsewhere as spring water. In the second process, the water, warmed by the rays of the sun becomes so light that it rises into the atmosphere in the form of water vapour and rejoices in the clarity; it purifies itself by evaporating and then falls once again on the earth as dew or as rain, bringing life to all vegetation. The same two methods of purification exist for men: those who do not wish to purify themselves by the rays of the sun will have to descend underground (symbolically speaking), passing through dark places, through suffering and undergoing severe pressure. Disciples, however, choose the second method: they expose themselves to the rays of the spiritual Sun and they rise up to absorb the most luminous elements which then purify them.

Read, mark, learn and inwardly digest these few words which I have said to you today. Link the name of God and the name of Jesus to the

"This is life eternal..."

five senses. Learn to work with your five senses and you will see how these words of Jesus will become more and more clear and accessible to you. "This is life eternal, that they might know thee, the only true God and Jesus Christ, whom thou hast sent." Knowing God is nothing other than being able to vibrate in unison with God, in perfect harmony with His thoughts, His feelings and His acts... and since God is eternal, man becomes eternal, like Him. This knowledge becomes Eternal Life, the highest state of consciousness.

II

"I am the vine, ye are the branches: He that abideth in me, and I in him, the same bringeth forth much fruit: for without me ye can do nothing. If a man abide not in me, he is cast forth as a branch and is withered: and men gather them and cast them into the fire and they are burned." All that is dead is thrown onto the fire in order that it may once again be vivified. The vine with its branches is a symbol of the human soul linked to God, drawing its strength from God Himself, from the Source. Just as the leaf pulled from the tree dies and rots away, so the soul detached from God becomes steadily weaker until it disappears. However, the soul which stays attached to the Tree grows and flourishes.

Time and eternity can be explained by these images of the vine and the tree. Eternity, Immensity, is the vine, God Himself. Time is all those little seeds which fall from eternity, those little leaves which break off, falling to the ground where they disappear; time is made up of all these moments, all these seconds which detach themselves from this tree which is eternity. So, therefore, time is always limited, always reduced and diminished; even stretches of millions and billions of years are still no more than a very short moment, belonging merely to limited time and everything which is limited always dies.

That is why man, seen as spirit, should not attach himself to time, otherwise he will always be limited, weak and will die. He must therefore forget time in order to embrace eternity, because then life will always flow in him, that abundant eternal life of which Jesus spoke when he said, "This is life eternal, that they might know thee the only true God". Eternal life then, is to link oneself to God so that His Life, the one and only true life can begin to circulate within us. Time, on the other hand, is all those moments that detach themselves; that is why we say that it is impossible to recapture time past as it is already lost.

Eternal life is a state of consciousness which it is possible for us to enter immediately and instantly. As soon as man manages to live and think in a divine way, as soon as he links himself to the Source, he is no longer separated from the Whole and so eternal life circulates within him.

Eternal life, then, is a quality of life, an especial degree of life, whereas life contained in time, transitory, unstable, fleeting and detached as it is, is no more than a particle containing the tiniest amount of energy, rather like the amputated tail of a lizard which goes on wriggling for a brief moment after it has been cut from the body.

When you link yourself to the Lord, to that Being who has no beginning and no end, your consciousness grows, it becomes luminous, vibrating in a quite different way and new life, the life of eternity, circulates within. You may question this, "Eternity, isn't that time that lasts forever?..." No, not necessarily... the present moment can be an eternity. Even though you are not going to live forever, you can still live eternal life. You cannot exhaust eternity, neither in the past nor in the future, but you are living in the present and each moment of this present can become eternity. It is very difficult to explain because I am speaking of a reality which belongs to the fourth and fifth dimension and in the third dimension, which is where words are found, we have nothing capable of expressing eternity. I use images to try to help you understand but, in fact, it is impossible to explain eternity because the limitless cannot be measured with a limited measure. However, despite this difficulty, I tell

"This is life eternal..."

you that the single fact of linking yourself to eternity can make a limited moment of time become eternity.

Let me give you another image. You see my stick: it is a straight line which has a beginning and an end, so clearly it is something limited, and therefore cannot be used to measure eternity. Suppose now that this stick was flexible and that I was able to bend it so that both ends met. It would then become a circle and with this circle I can express eternity: no beginning, no end, no bits and pieces... just infinite unity. So then each moment of time, each second in which I manage to make that connection to the source, to infinity, becomes eternity; by entering the circle each moment changes its nature, changes its quality, it is no longer a detached portion of the Whole. Each point of the straight line is a point in time, whereas each point in the circle is a point in eternity; that is why each second in which I connect to the Source enters the circle of eternity.

In order to blossom, each branch must be connected to the source, to the vine, then from the nourishment it receives it will be able to produce flowers and fruit. Therefore link yourselves to the divine principle, to Christ, in order to live the life of Christ, in order to transform your limited, personal, purely human awareness into an unlimited consciousness, a universal consciousness, so that a single consciousness becomes the consciousness of eternity. Do not go on thinking about time, about your cares and sorrows, forget your imperfections and your deficiencies... just concern yourself with the centre, concern yourself with the divine principle that is within you; immerse yourself in eternal life, live the life of eternity. From now on, you can live eternal life, since it is no longer a question of duration of time, it is not necessary to live billions of years to experience eternity. Besides, even if you lived billions of years that would still not be eternity because, as I have said, eternity is not a duration of time, it is a state of consciousness.

Time is no more than anarchic particles which want to detach themselves from the tree of eternity to establish their own kingdom! The particles detach themselves, live for a certain time, which is why they are called time and then they die. Even supposing that all these particles which became detached one after another were able to link together into billions of years, they would never be able to form eternity because there would always be a beginning and an end to the chain. Eternal life is something quite different, it is a quality of life, an intensity of life, and if you manage to live this intensity of life, even for a fraction of a second, you enter eternity.

"This is life eternal..."

Today, I give you a key which can be found in the two sayings of Christ, "I am the vine, ye are the branches", and, "This is life eternal, that they might know thee the only true God". In two different forms the same truth is expressed: man must find the path in order to link himself once again to the divine source and once connected he must never separate himself, for separation leads to spiritual and physical death. Everything in Nature can help link us to the Source, but the most powerful, the most efficient connection is the sun. The sun is the symbol of this living river which flows down to us, which sparkles forth, flooding the whole universe: it is the symbol of God. It is the sun who best can help us to rediscover the path towards the Creator, to live, to vibrate like Him, to become the branch linked to the vine. The sun is the vine, and if we become its branches we will have eternal life.

In ancient texts Initiates represented the snake in three different ways: undulating in a sinusoidal manner, or curled up in a spiral, or in the form of a circle – the serpent swallowing its tail. These three different images are very profound symbols. The snake is presented in the Bible as the subtlest of all beasts, the most intelligent, but it is also the personification of evil and trickery. Another time, if you wish, I will explain. Today we will dwell on these three representations of the snake I have just mentioned, for they symbolize the work of the disciple who has to be able to sublimate the snake, or to transform the straight line into a circle. To do this requires a psychic, intellectual process, an initiatic process.

The serpent is first of all a straight line, symbolically speaking (in reality it is a sinusoid), it creeps along the ground. Then it holds itself up vertically, it takes the shape of a spiral, and that is the spinal column. Finally it must join its two extremities, its head and tail, to form a circle, so entering into harmonious and symmetric movement, the creative movement of eternity. All emanations, all energies are then evenly distributed and organized and there are no more struggles, there is no more disharmony amongst them; all points on the periphery are equidistant from the centre and so can produce sublime patterns of interaction. The Initiate who can make that circle within himself becomes powerful, inexhaustible, perfect like the sun; he lives in eternity.

The straight line, therefore, must become a circle. Physicists see the straight line as part of a circle. Given the fact that everything moves, that there are only curved lines in space, the straight

"This is life eternal..."

line does not exist. Seen in spiritual terms, man must become a circle. Look at a child: before he is born he is all curled up on himself, like a ball. You may say that that is just an efficient way of taking up the least amount of space in his mother's womb. That is a possible interpretation.... Then after his birth he learns to stand upright. Spiritually speaking, the reverse happens as he must take the shape of the circle, that is to say, he must leave his limited personal awareness in order to live the cosmic life, the universal life, the life of eternity.

In fact, nothing and nobody can detach themselves from the universal life: not even the smallest speck of dust, the tiniest atom, can escape from cosmic life. The break is made only in the consciousness of beings and after that, of course, all sorts of disorders follow on other planes. In the midst of all these disorders one is obviously still linked to the cosmos, but only to its lower regions. Therefore the one thing that needs to be done is to change the region, to change the levels. In a house you can decide to live on the higher levels or on the lower ones... you can even choose to live in the cellar. It is, however, an illusion to believe that you can detach yourself totally: nobody has ever succeeded in detaching himself from the influences of the cosmic forces and energies. You can change your conditions, you can move into different regions which may be more or less agreeable but all these changes affect your awareness and that affects everything else. That is why I keep insisting, "Go up to the summit, go back to the Source!" Each day, whatever you are doing, whether you are eating, walking or working, think of linking yourself to the Source, think endlessly of re-establishing your connection with the divine principle which is in you, because that is living eternal life.

No book can teach us more essential truths than the Gospels. You may argue, "We have already read them and we found nothing in them.... That is why we are now looking at other religions: Chinese, Japanese, Indian, Moslem...." Well, that's fine, but that is simply because you have understood nothing of the incommensurable wisdom which is to be found in the Gospels; these were written for you and yet you go off to look for the light in teachings which were not intended for you! Yes, I know, you can get saturated with texts that are so well known and you long to change your food a little. However it is dangerous to go looking for it in teachings which you do not understand, which were not made for your structure, for your mentality. What is right for you is the teaching of

Christ. You have neither read it seriously, nor meditated on it. You look for something else, that's true, but why, for what reason? Very often people follow an Oriental teaching to parade in front of others, to throw dust in their eyes or quite simply, to feel important in their own eyes. This does no good at all, it only goes to show that you prefer exaggerations to the simple truth. You abandon Christ... but whom do you put in His place?

By the same author:

Izvor Collection

201 – TOWARD A SOLAR CIVILISATION

Although we may know about heliocentricity from the point of view of astronomy, we are still far from having exhausted all its possibilities in the biological, psychological, cultural and spiritual spheres. We are constantly looking for more effective ways of harnessing solar energy: why not look for traces of the sun buried deep in man's psychic structure and consequently in human society? The sun exists within each one of us and if allowed to, can manifest its presence by awakening our consciousness to a global view of human problems.

202 – MAN, MASTER OF HIS DESTINY

Why is one born in a particular country and a particular family? Why is one healthy, rich, illustrious and powerful, or on the contrary poor, handicapped and miserable? The bonds one forges with others almost without realizing it, where do they spring from and why? Even those who think they are entirely free must put up with their fate because of their ignorance of the laws which govern the invisible world. By revealing these laws, the Master not only helps the disciple to unravel the tangled threads of his life, he also gives him the tools he must have in order to become master of his own destiny.

203 – EDUCATION BEGINS BEFORE BIRTH

Is it possible for education to begin before birth? Yes. Because true education is primarily subconscious. A child is not a little animal which you can start training as soon as it is old enough. A child in the womb is a soul and its mother can have a beneficial influence on it even at this stage, through the harmony of her thoughts, acts and feelings. And this pre-natal influence which, in essence, is a form of magic, must be faithfully continued once the baby is born, for, as all parents should realize, a tiny baby is highly sensitive to both its physical and spiritual environment. It is by their own example that parents and teachers can best succeed in their task of educating the child. He is far more deeply impressed by the way the people around him behave and are, than by any lesson or advice that he receives from time to time. Educating the child's subconscious requires a very high level of consciousness on the part of the educators.

204 – THE YOGA OF NUTRITION

This book is not a dietary handbook, it has nothing to do with diet. The Master Omraam Mikhaël Aïvanhov considers the way man thinks about the food more important than what, or how much, he eats. The Master lifts the act of eating onto the level of a mystical rite, a sacrament such as Holy Communion, the Last Supper, in all their spiritual significance.

Even someone to whom the spiritual aspect is foreign cannot but understand as he reads that his thoughts and feelings, his way of considering his daily nourishment, are what lead him to the profound mysteries of the relationship between man and Nature, the nature which nourishes him. If he deepens that relationship by extracting from the food the more subtle, finer elements, his entire being will then be able to unfold and flourish.

205 – SEXUAL FORCE OR THE WINGED DRAGON

The dragon, fabulous beast of Mythology and all Christian iconography, is not merely a relic of antiquity but a symbol of the human being's instinctive, primitive forces. The spiritual life is the process of learning how to subdue, control and direct these forces so that man will be propelled to the highest peaks of spirituality. The fire-breathing monster with the tail of a serpent has wings as well, indicating that the forces he embodies have a spiritual destination. The Master Omraam Mikhaël Aïvanhov says, "Sexual energy can be compared to petrol: if you are ignorant and careless you are burned by it, your very quintessence will be destroyed by this consuming force. The Initiates are those whose knowledge permits them to use the force to soar above the universe." That is the true meaning of the winged Dragon.

206 – THE UNIVERSAL WHITE BROTHERHOOD IS NOT A SECT

The very strong feelings of antipathy held by many of the general public on the subject of sects tend to hide the real problems of society. Indignation is felt against minorities who have decided to undertake a spiritual life apart from orthodox religious practice but non-conformity in other fields is looked upon with favour. The intellectual, political, social and economic fields are largely composed of many separate parts and groups which are, in effect, 'sects,' concerned with the triumph of their own particular theories or interests over those of their opponents. From now on a sect will no longer be defined in relation to the official church but in terms of the universality of its ideas in all fields. And if the Universal White Brotherhood is not a sect, it is precisely because its Teaching, which is directed to men of every race and religion and which encompasses every kind of human activity, aims at developing a consciousness of universality amongst all men.

207 – WHAT IS A SPIRITUAL MASTER?

Although the idea of a spiritual Master is becoming more and more familiar to the public, the nature and role of a Master are still poorly understood, even by those who claim to be disciples. The purpose of this book is essentially to shed light on the subject. This clarification may seem ruthless to some, but it is necessary, for what matters above all is not to delude oneself as to the realities of the spiritual life. It is true that a Master is that prodigious being capable of leading men towards the highest summits of the spirit, but for the Master as for his disciples, this exciting adventure can be successful only if it is accompanied by tremendous demands upon oneself.

208 – UNDER THE DOVE, THE REIGN OF PEACE

All the official steps taken in favour of peace seem to infer that it is a state which can be imposed on men from the outside... the creating of organizations for peace, reinforcing security means, the imprisonment or pure and simple suppression of troublemakers, for example. But what hope is there for peace when man continues to nourish within himself the seeds of all political, social and economic conflicts? These seeds are his uncontrolled desires for possession and domination. A better understanding of what peace truly is and the conditions necessary for achieving it are called for. As long as man doesn't make the decision to intervene on the battlefield of his disorderly thoughts and feelings, he won't be able to create a lasting peace.

209 – CHRISTMAS AND EASTER IN THE INITIATIC TRADITION

The Feasts of Christmas and Easter, celebrated annually throughout Christendom to commemorate the birth and resurrection of Jesus, actually are part of the initiatic tradition in existence long before the Christian era. Their appearance at those particular times of the year – the Winter solstice and the Spring equinox – is indicative of their Cosmic significance and also of the fact that man participates in the processes of gestation, birth and blossoming which take place in nature.

Christmas and Easter, the second birth and the resurrection, are really two different ways of celebrating the regeneration of man and his birth into the spiritual world.

210 – THE TREE OF THE KNOWLEDGE OF GOOD AND EVIL

The existence of evil in a world created by God who is perfect is an enigma which remains unsolved to this day by the world's philosophies or religions. Within the framework of Judeo-Christianism, Master Omraam Mikhaël Aïvanhov asserts that the solution lies in knowing what methods to use to contain evil, rather than in explanations or interpretations. Whatever its origin, evil is a reality which man confronts daily, both inwardly and outwardly. He must learn to deal with it. For him to fight against it is useless, even dangerous, for the odds are against him. He must be armed with *methods* of dealing with it, to overcome and transform it. This book offers those methods.

211 – FREEDOM, THE SPIRIT TRIUMPHANT

Freedom has become such a political stake that we have lost sight of the true terms through which man can find freedom. It is those terms, which are those of the relationship between spirit and matter, that the Master Omraam Mikhaël Aïvanhov attempts to restore. "No creature," he says, "can subsist without a certain number of elements that he receives from outside himself. God alone is not subject to this law; He has no need of anything external to Himself. But He has left a spark of Himself, a spirit identical to Him in nature, in every human being, and therefore man, thanks to his spirit, can create everything he needs. The Teaching I bring is that of the spirit, the Creator, and not that of matter and of creation. This is why I tell you that by entering the realm of the spirit which creates, forms and shapes matter, we will escape the hold the outside world has on us and be free."

212 – LIGHT IS A LIVING SPIRIT

Light offers infinite possibilities to us in the material and spiritual fields. It is seen by tradition as the living substance with which God created the world and in the last few years we have seen the development of the laser with all its potential. Omraam Mikhaël Aïvanhov invites us in this book to discover light's spiritual possibilities, to see how it can protect, nourish and teach us to know ourselves, nature and God, but above all he shows light as the only truly effective method of transforming ourselves and the world.

213 – MAN'S TWO NATURES, HUMAN AND DIVINE

To justify their failings and weaknesses, you hear people exclaim, "I'm only human!" What they should actually be saying is, "I'm only animal!" How, then, should we define human nature?

Man, that ambiguous creature placed by evolution on the border between the animal world and the divine world, has a double nature. To be able to advance further in his evolution he must become aware of this ambivalence. It says in the Holy Writ, "Ye are gods," which ought to remind man of the presence within of the higher essence which he must learn to manifest. "That is the real meaning of destiny," says Master Omraam Mikhaël Aïvanhov, "the true purpose and goal of our existence." This is why he comes back again and again to this question, giving us methods for us to learn and use in order to manifest ourselves as the gods we really are... but do not know yet.

214 – HOPE FOR THE WORLD: SPIRITUAL GALVANOPLASTY

"Everything in the universe, in Nature and in man reflects the two fundamental principles, masculine and feminine. All Creation is the result of the two principles working together as a reflection of the creative cosmic principles, our Heavenly Father and our Divine Mother, Nature. Everywhere the two principles are at work, in Nature and in man, whose mind and spirit represent the male principle and whose heart and soul represent the feminine principle. One cannot work without the other, they are not productive when separated... which explains why men and women are constantly seeking each other.

Spiritual Galvanoplasty is the science of the two principles applied to man's inner life."

Omraam Mikhaël Aïvanhov

215 – THE TRUE MEANING OF CHRIST'S TEACHING

In his lectures over the years, some of which form the contents of this book, the Maître Omraam Mikhaël Aïvanhov shows that Jesus condensed his entire Teaching into the prayer beginning with the words, "Our Father which art in heaven..." now called the Lord's Prayer. Initiates, says the Master, proceed as Nature does. A tree with its roots and trunk, branches, leaves, blossoms and fruit at first is no more than a minute seed but, if you plant it, water it and expose it to the sun, it becomes a majestic tree in all its splendour... because Nature in her wonderful way has condensed the tree's entire potential into the tiny seed. Jesus did the same. He took his Teaching, the new Science he was bringing mankind, and condensed it into a prayer to his Father in the hope that this seed would take root in men's souls, be nurtured by them with care, and grow into its potential: the massive, fruitful tree of the Initiatic Science, the real Teaching of Christ.

Omraam Mikhaël Aïvanhov

216 – THE LIVING BOOK OF NATURE

"We live in a civilisation which requires us to know how to read and write, and this is very good. It will always be necessary to read and write but we must also know how to do so on other planes. In Initiatic Science, to read means to be able to decipher the subtle and hidden side of objects and creatures, to interpret the symbols and signs placed everywhere by Cosmic Intelligence in the great book of the universe. To write means to leave one's imprint on this great book, to act upon stones, plants, animals and men through the magic force of one's spirit. It is not just on paper that we must know how to read and write but upon all regions of the universe."

Omraam Mikhaël Aïvanhov

Distributed by:

AUSTRIA	HELMUTH FELDER VERLAG Kranebitterallee 88/144 – Postfach 33 A-6027 Innsbruck
BELGIUM	VANDER S.A. – Av. des Volontaires 321 B - 1150 Bruxelles
BRITISH ISLES	PROSVETA Ltd. – 4 St. Helena Terrace Richmond, Surrey TW9 1NR Trade orders to: ELEMENT Books Ltd Unit 25 Longmead Shaftesbury Dorset SP7 8PL
CANADA	PROSVETA Inc. – 1565 Montée Masson Duvernay est, Laval, Qué. H7E 4P2
DENMARK	SANKT ANSGARS FORLAG Bredgade 67 DK – 1260 COPENHAGUE
FRANCE	Editions PROSVETA S.A. – B.P. 12 83601 Fréjus Cedex
GERMANY	URANIA – Rudolf Diesel Ring 26 D - 8029 Sauerlach
GREECE	PROSVETA HELLAS 90 Bd. Iroon Polytechniou – 185 36 Le Pirée
HOLLAND	MAKLU B.V. – Koninginnelaan 96 NL - 7315 EB Apeldoorn
HONG KONG	HELIOS 31 New Kap Bin Long Village Sai Kung N.T., Hong Kong
IRELAND	PROSVETA IRL. 84 Irishtown – Clonmel
ITALY	PROSVETA – Bastelli 7 I - 43036 Fidenza (Parma)
PORTUGAL	Edições IDADE D'OURO Rua Passos Manuel 20 – 3.° Esq. P - 1100 Lisboa
SPAIN	PROSVETA ESPAÑOLA – Caspe 41 Barcelona – 10
SWITZERLAND	PROSVETA Société Coopérative CH - 1801 Les Monts-de-Corsier
UNITED-STATES	PROSVETA U.S.A. – P.O. Box 49614 Los Angeles, California 90049

Enquiries should be addressed to the nearest distributor

PRINTED IN FRANCE
JULY 1985
PROSVETA EDITIONS, FRÉJUS

– N° d'impression : 1422 –
Dépôt légal : Juillet 1985
Printed in France